A QUICK GUIDE TO C# WITH UNITY

Get Started with C# in Unity in less than 60 minutes.

Patrick Felicia

Credits

A QUICK GUIDE TO C# WITH UNITY

Copyright © 2017 Patrick Felicia

All rights reserved. No part of this book may be reproduced, stored in retrieval systems, or transmitted in any form or by any means, without the prior written permission of the publisher (Patrick Felicia), except in the case of brief quotations embedded in critical articles or reviews.

Every effort has been made in the preparation of this book to ensure the accuracy of the information presented. However, the information contained in this book is sold without warranty, either expressed or implied. Neither the author and its dealers and distributors will be held liable for any damages caused or alleged to be caused directly or indirectly by this book.

First published: August 2017

Published by Patrick Felicia

CREDITS

Author: Patrick Felicia

About the Author

Patrick Felicia is a lecturer and researcher at Waterford Institute of Technology, where he teaches and supervises undergraduate and postgraduate students. He obtained his MSc in Multimedia Technology in 2003 and PhD in Computer Science in 2009 from University College Cork, Ireland.

He has published several books and articles on the use of video games for educational purposes, including the Handbook of Research on Improving Learning and Motivation through Educational Games: Multidisciplinary Approaches (published by IGI), and Digital Games in Schools: A Handbook for Teachers, published by European Schoolnet.

Patrick has published over 10 books on Unity, covering several key skills such as C# and JavaScript in Unity, 3D and 2D game development with Unity, as well as 3D Character Animation.

Patrick is also the Editor-in-chief of the International Journal of Game-Based Learning (IJGBL), and the Conference Director of the Irish Conference on Game-Based Learning, a popular conference on games and learning organized throughout Ireland.

BOOKS FROM THE SAME AUTHOR

Unity 5 from Zero to Proficiency (Foundations)

In this book, you will become more comfortable with Unity's interface and its core features by creating a project that includes both an indoor and an outdoor environment. This book only covers drag and drop features, so that you are comfortable with Unity's interface before starting to code (in the next book). After completing this book, you will be able to create outdoors environments with terrains and include water, hills, valleys, sky-boxes, use built-in controllers (First- and Third-Person controllers) to walk around the 3D environment and also add and pilot a car and an aircraft.

Books from the same author

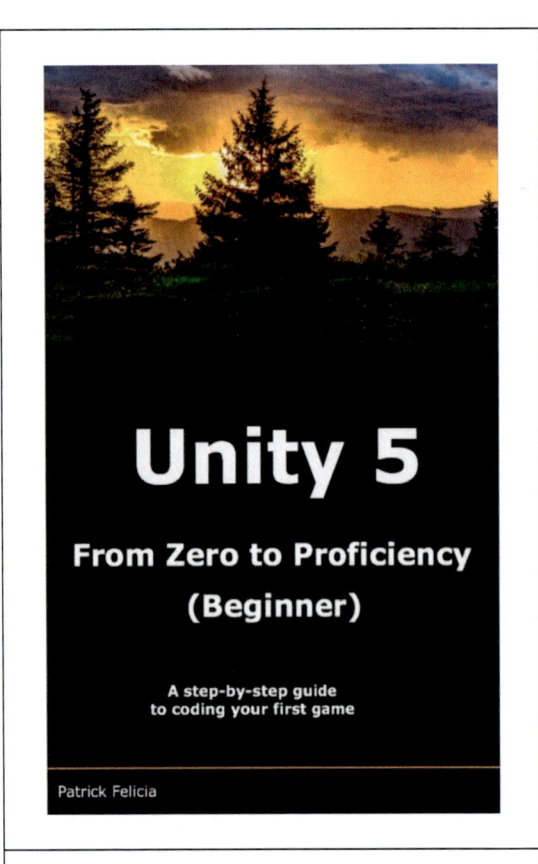

Unity 5 from Zero to Proficiency (Beginner)

In this book, you will get started with coding using JavaScript. The book provides an introduction to coding for those with no previous programming experience, and it explains how to use JavaScript in order to create an interactive environment. Throughout the book, you will be creating a game, and also implementing the core mechanics through scripting. After completing this book you will be able to write code in JavaScript, understand and apply key programming principles, understand and avoid common coding mistakes, learn and apply best programming practices, and build solid programming skills.

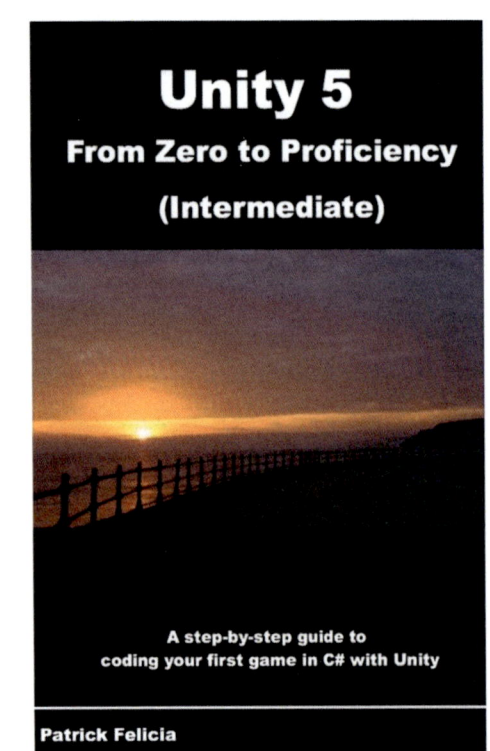

Unity 5 from Zero to Proficiency (Intermediate)

In this book, you improve your coding skills and learn more programming concepts to add more activity to your game while optimizing your code. The book provides an introduction to coding in C# t. Throughout the book, you will be creating a game, and also implementing the core mechanics through scripting.

After completing this book you will be able to write code in C#, understand and apply Object-Oriented Programming techniques in C#, create and use your own classes, use Unity's Finite State Machines, and apply intermediate Artificial Intelligence.

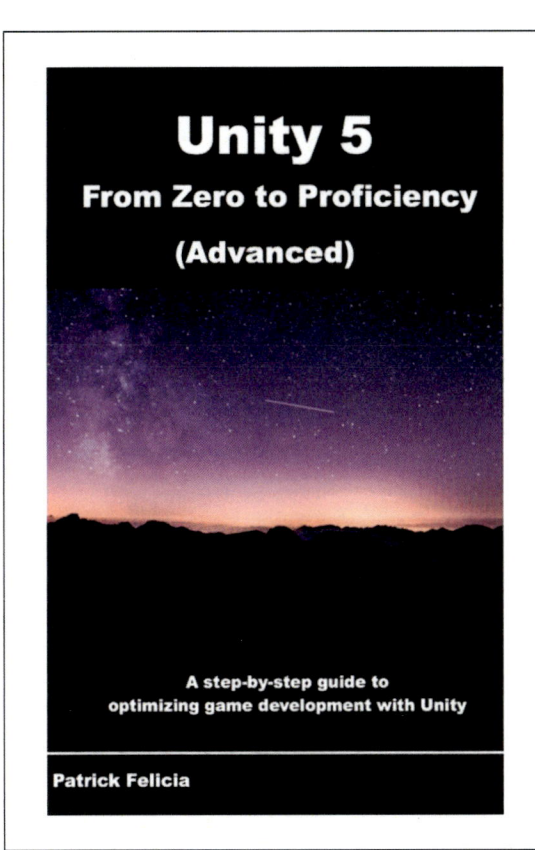

Unity 5 from Zero to Proficiency (Advanced)

In this book, which is the last in the series, you will go from Intermediate to Advanced and get to work on more specific topics to improve your games and their performances.

After completing this book, you will be able to create a (networked) multi-player game, access Databases from Unity, understand and apply key design, patterns for game development, use your time more efficiently to create games, structure and manage a Unity project efficiently, optimize game performances, optimize the structure of your game, and create levels procedurally.

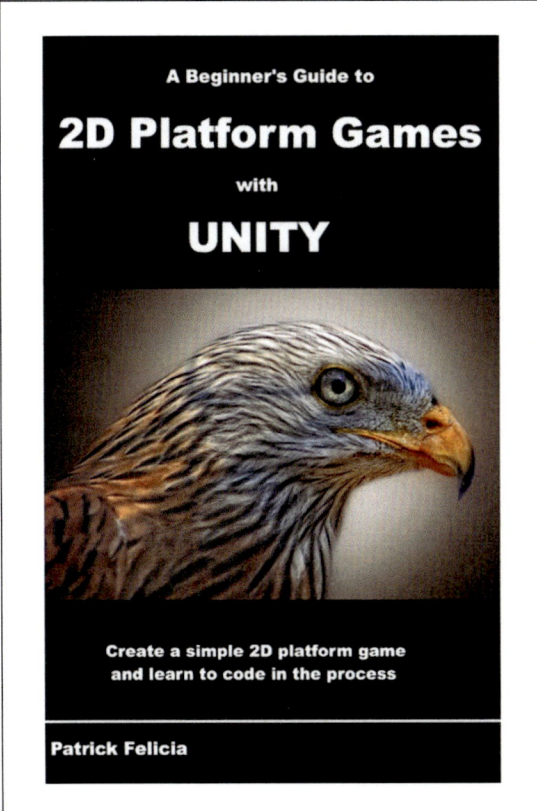

A Beginner's Guide to 2D Platform Games with Unity

In this book, you will get started with creating a simple 2D platform game. The book provides an introduction to platform games, and it explains how to use C# in order to create an interactive environment.

Books from the same author

	A Beginner's Guide to 2D Shooter Games with Unity In this book, you will get started with creating a simple 2D shooter game. The book provides an introduction to 2D shooter games, and it explains how to use C# in order to create an interactive environment
	A Beginner's Guide to 2D Puzzle Games with Unity In this book, you will get started with creating four different types of puzzle games. The book provides an introduction to 2D puzzle games, and it explains how to use C# in order to create four addictive types of puzzle games including: word games (i.e., hangman), memory game (i.e., simon game), card matching game, and a puzzle.

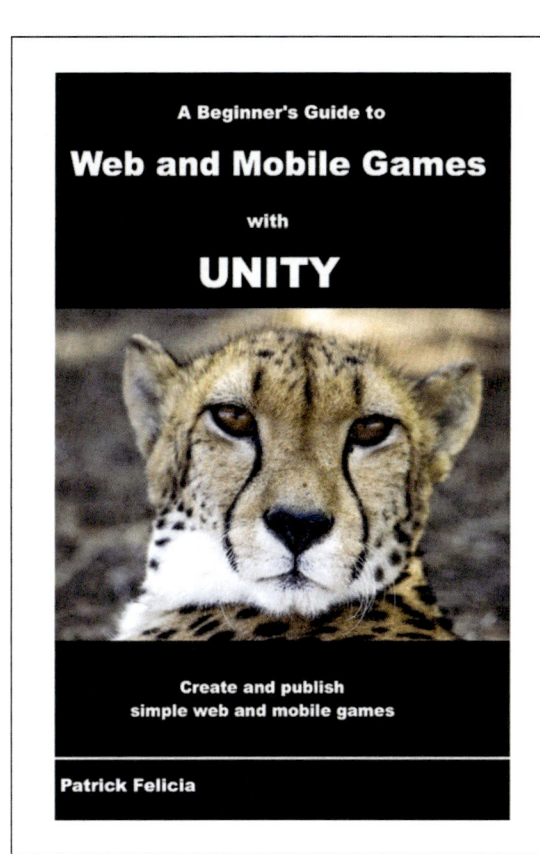

A Beginner's Guide to Web and Mobile Games with Unity

In this book, you will get started with exporting a simple infinite runner to the web and Android. The book provides an introduction to how to export and share your game with friends on the Web and on Android Play. It provides step-by-step instructions and explains how to easily share a simple game with your friends so that they can play it on your site or an Android device including: processing taps, exporting the game to a web page, debugging your app, signing your app, and much more.

SUPPORT AND RESOURCES FOR THIS BOOK

So that you can complete the project presented in this book seamlessly, a website has been setup, and it includes all the material you need to complete the project presented in the next chapters (e.g., textures or solutions for each chapter), as well as bonus material.

To avail of this content, you can open the link:

http://www.learntocreategames.com/books/.

http://www.learntocreategames.com also provides you with the opportunity to subscribe to a newsletter, obtain exclusive discounts and offers on new books, and gain access to video tutorials on creating games.

Why should you subscribe?

- Be the first to be notified of new resources available.
- Receive regular updates and tutorials on creating games.
- Receive a newsletter with tips and hints on game development.

This book is dedicated to Helena

TABLE OF CONTENTS

1 Introduction to Programming in C# 2
   Why use C# instead of JavaScript 3
   Introduction 4
   Statements 6
   Comments 8
   Variables 10
   Arrays 12
   Constants 15
   Operators 17
   Conditional statements 18
   Switch Statements 19
   Loops 21
   Classes 24
   Defining a class 25
   Accessing class members and variables 27
   Constructors 31
   Destructors 33
   Static members of a class 34
   Inheritance 37
   Methods 41
   Accessing methods and access modifiers 43
   Common methods 44
   Scope of variables 45
   Events 47
   Polymorphism (general concepts) 48
   Dynamic polymorphism 49
   Workflow to create a script 52
   How scripts are compiled 53
   Coding Convention 54
   A few things to remember when you create a script (checklist) 55

2 Creating your First Script 57
   Getting started 58
   Creating your first method 69
   Creating your own class 75
   Common errors and their meaning 80
   Best practices 83

3 Frequently Asked Questions 84
   C# Scripts 85

4 Thank you 87

PREFACE

To be able to help people like you, I have designed and published more than 8 books on Unity; these books are in-depth and really provide a significant amount of information on a wide range of topics related to Unity, including 2D/3D game development, Artificial Intelligence, Animation, and much more...

This being said, while these books are comprehensive, many readers, like you, may just want to focus on a particular topic and get started fast.

This book is part of a series entitled **A Quick Guide To**, and does just this. In this book series, you have the opportunity to get started on a particular topic in less than 60 minutes, delving right into the information that you really need. Of course, you can, after reading this book, move-on to more comprehensive books; however, I understand that sometimes you may have little time to complete a project and that you need to get comfortable with a topic fast.

In this book entitled "**A Quick Guide to C# with Unity**" you will discover how to quickly get started programming in C# with Unity, including C# concepts and how they apply within Unity.

WHAT YOU NEED TO USE THIS BOOK

To complete the project presented in this book, you only need Unity 5.0 (or a more recent version) and to also ensure that your computer and its operating system comply with Unity's requirements. Unity can be downloaded from the official website (http://www.unity3d.com/download), and before downloading, you can check that your computer is up to scratch on the following page: http://www.unity3d.com/unity/system-requirements. At the time of writing this book, the following operating systems are supported by Unity for development: Windows XP (i.e., SP2+, 7 SP1+), Windows 8, and Mac OS X 10.6+. In terms of graphics card, most cards produced after 2004 should be suitable.

In terms of computer skills, all knowledge introduced in this book will assume no prior programming experience from the reader. So for now, you only need to be able to perform common computer tasks such as downloading items, opening and saving files, and be comfortable with dragging and dropping items and typing.

WHO THIS BOOK IS FOR

If you can answer **yes** to all these questions, then this book is for you:

1. Are you a total beginner in C#?

2. Would you like to get started with C# and create interactive games with Unity?

3. Would you like to start creating great 3D games?

4. Although you may have had some prior exposure to Unity, would you like to into how C# can be linked to scenes and objects?

If you can answer yes to all these questions, then this book is **not** for you:

1. Can you already easily create a game in C#?

2. Are you looking for a reference book on Unity programming?

3. Are you an experienced (or at least advanced) Unity programmer?

If you can answer yes to all three questions, you may instead look for the next books in the series. To see the content and topics covered by these books, you can check the official website (www.learntocreategames.com/books).

IMPROVING THE BOOK

Although great care was taken in checking the content of this book, I am human, and some errors could remain in the book. As a result, it would be great if you could let me know of any issue or error you may have come across in this book, so that it can be solved and the book updated accordingly. To report an error, you can email me (learntocreategames@gmail.com) with the following information:

- Name of the book.

- The page where the error was detected.

- Describe the error and also what you think the correction should be.

Once your email is received, the error will be checked, and, in the case of a valid error, it will be corrected and the book page will be updated to reflect the changes accordingly.

SUPPORTING THE AUTHOR

A lot of work has gone into this book and it is the fruit of long hours of preparation, brainstorming, and finally writing. As a result, I would ask that you do not distribute any illegal copies of this book.

This means that if a friend wants a copy of this book, s/he will have to buy it through the official channels (i.e., through Amazon, lulu.com, or the book's official website: www.learntocreategames.com/learn-unity-ebook).

If some of your friends are interested in the book, you can refer them to the book's official website (http://www.learntocreategames.com/learn-unity-ebook) where they can either buy the book, enter a monthly draw to be in for a chance of receiving a free copy of the book, or to be notified of future promotional offers.

1

INTRODUCTION TO PROGRAMMING IN C#

In this section we will discover C# programming principles and concepts, so that you can start programming in the next chapter. If you have already coded using C# (or a similar language), you can skip this chapter.

After completing this chapter, you will be able to:

- Understand key differences between UnityScript and C#.
- Understand the reasons why you need to consider C#.
- Understand object-oriented programming (OOP) concepts when coding in C#.
- Get used to and understand the concepts of variables, methods, and scope.
- Understand key best practices for coding, particularly in C#.
- Understand conditional statements and decision making structures.
- Understand the concept of loops.

WHY USE C# INSTEAD OF JAVASCRIPT

While UnityScript is great to start scripting with game development in Unity, it is also quite different from the JavaScript used for the web, for example. So it does help you to understand some key programming concepts, but it may be challenging to transfer this skill to a different platform. On the other hand, by learning C# within Unity, you get to discover a new language that is object-oriented, relatively easy to learn, and with strong resemblances with Java (another widespread object-oriented language). So while JavaScript makes sense at the start of your journey through Unity, it is also a good idea to move on to C# and develop skills that you will be able to transfer to other platforms and programming languages. Another advantage of using C# is that it may be a good asset if you would like to pursue a career in the gaming industry, as many gaming companies use this language instead of UnityScript.

Introduction to Programming in C#

INTRODUCTION

When scripting in Unity, you are communicating with the Game Engine and asking it to perform actions. To communicate with the system, you are using a language or a set of words bound by a syntax that the computer and you know. This language consists of keywords, key phrases, and a syntax that ensures that the instructions are understood properly. In computer science, this sentence needs to be exact, precise, unambiguous, and with a correct syntax. In other words, it needs to be **exact**. The syntax is a set of rules that are followed when writing code in C# (as for JavaScript). In addition to its syntax, C# programming also uses classes; so your scripts will be saved as classes.

In the next section, we will learn how to use this syntax. If you have already coded in JavaScript, some of the information provided in the rest of this chapter may look familiar and this prior exposure to JavaScript will definitely help you. This being said, UnityScript and C#, despite some relative similarities, are quite different in many aspects (e.g., variable declaration, function declaration, etc.).

When scripting in C#, you will be using a combination of the following:

- Classes.
- Objects.
- Statements.
- Comments.
- Variables.
- Constants.
- Operators.
- Assignments.
- Data types.
- Methods.
- Decision making structures.
- Loops.
- Inheritance (more advanced).
- Polymorphism (more advanced).
- Operator overloading (more advanced).

- Interfaces.
- Name spaces.
- Events.
- Comparisons.
- Type conversions.
- Reserved words.
- Messages to the console windows.
- Declarations.
- Calls to methods.

The list may look a bit intimidating but, not to worry, we will explore these in the next sections, and you will get to know and use them smoothly using hands-on examples.

Introduction to Programming in C#

STATEMENTS

When you write a piece of C# code, you need to tell the system to execute your instructions (e.g., print information) using statements. A statement is literally an order or something you ask the system to do. For example, in the next line of code, the statement will tell Unity to print a message in the **Console** window:

```
print ("Hello Word");
```

When writing statements, there are a few rules that you need to know:

- Order of statements: each statement is executed in the order it appears in the script. For example, in the next example, the code will print **hello**, then **world**; this is because the associated statements are in that particular sequence.

```
print ("hello");
print ("world");
```

- Statements are separated by **semi-colons** (i.e., semi-colon at the end of each statement).

Note that several statements can be added on the same line, as long as they are separated by a semi-colon.

- For example the next line of code has a correct syntax.

```
print("hello");print ("world");
```

- Multiple spaces are ignored for statements; however, it is good practice to add spaces around the operators such as +, -, /, or % for clarity. For example, in the next example, we say that **a** is equal to **b**. There is a space both before and after the operator =.

```
a = b;
```

- Statements to be executed together (e.g., based on the same condition) can be grouped using what is usually referred to as **code blocks**. In C# (as for JavaScript), code blocks are symbolized by curly brackets (e.g., { or }). So, in other words, if you needed to group several statements, we would include them all within the same curly brackets, as follows:

```
{
    print ("hello stranger!");
    print ("today, we will learn about scripting");
}
```

As we have seen earlier, a statement usually employs or starts with a keyword (i.e., a word that the computer knows). Each of these keywords has a specific purpose and the most common ones (at this stage) are used for:

- Printing a message in the **Console** window: the keyword is **print**.

- Declaring a variable: the keyword depends on the type of variable (e.g., **int** for integers, **string** for text, **bool** for Boolean variables, etc.) and we will see more about this in the next sections.

- Declaring a method: the keyword depends on the type of the data returned by the method. For example, in C#, the name of a method is preceded by the keyword **int** when the method returns an **integer**, **string** when the method returns a **string**, or **void** when the method does not return any information.

> What is called a **method** in C# is what used to be called a function in UnityScript; these terms (i.e., function and method) differ in at least two ways: in C# you need to specify the type of the data returned by this method, and the keyword **function** is not used anymore in C# for this purpose. We will see more about this topic in the next sections.

- Marking a block of instructions to be executed based on a condition: the keywords are **if…else**.

- Exiting a function: the keyword is **return**.

COMMENTS

In C# (similarly to JavaScript), you can use comments to explain the code and to make it more readable. This becomes important as the size of your code increases; and it is also important if you work as part of a team, so that team members can understand your code and make amendments in the right places, if and when it is needed.

When code is commented, it is not executed. There are two ways to comment your code in C#; you can use **single** or **multi-line** comments. In single-line comments, a **double forward slash** is added at the start of a line or after a statement, so that this line (or part thereof) is commented, as illustrated in the next code snippet.

```
//the next line prints Hello in the console window
print ("Hello");
//the next line declares the variable name
string name;
name = "Hello";//sets the value of the variable name
```

In multi-line comments, any text between /* and */ will be commented (and not executed). This is also refereed as **comment blocks**.

```
/* the next lines after the comments print hello in the console window
we then declare the variable name and assign a value
*/
print("Hello");
string name;
name = "Hello";//sets the value of the variable name
//print ("Hello World")
/*
    string name;
    name = "My Name";
*/
```

In addition to providing explanations about your code, you can also use comments to prevent part of your code to be executed. This is very useful when you would like to debug your code and find where the error or bug might be, using a very simple method. By commenting sections of your code, and using a process of elimination, you can usually find the issue quickly. For example, you can comment all the code and run the script; then comment half the code, and run the script. If it works, it means that the error is within the code that has been commented, and if it does not work, it means that the error is in the code that has not been commented. In the first case (if the code works), we could then just comment half of the portion of the code that has already been commented. So, by successively commenting more specific areas of our code, we can get to discover what part of the code includes the bug. This process is often called **dichotomy** (as we successively divide a code section into two). It is usually effective to debug your code because the number of iterations (dividing part of the code in two) is more predictable and also potentially less time-consuming. For example for 100 lines of codes, we can successively narrow down the issue to 50, 25, 12, 6, and 3 lines (5 to 6 iterations in this case would be necessary instead of going through the whole 100 lines).

VARIABLES

A variable is a container. It includes a value that may change overtime. When using variables, we usually need to: (1) declare the variable (by specifying its type), (2) assign a value to this variable, and (3) possibly combine this variable with other variables using operators.

```
int myAge;//we declare the variable
myAge = 20;// we set the variable to 20
myAge = myAge + 1; //we add 1 to the variable myAge
```

In the previous example, we have declared a variable **myAge**, its type is **int** (integer), we set it to **20** and we then add 1 to it.

> Note that, contrary to UnityScript where the keyword **var** is used to declare a variable, in C# the variable is declared using its type followed by its name. As we will see later we will also need to use what is called an **access modifier** in order to specify how this variable can be accessed.

> Note that in the previous code we have assigned the value **myAge + 1** to **myAge**; the = operator is an assignment operator; in other words, it is there to assign a value to a variable and is not to be understood in a strict algebraic sense (i.e., that the values or variables on both sides of the = sign are equal).

Contrary to UnityScript, and to make coding easier and leaner, in C# you can perform a multiple declaration of several variables of the same type in the same statement. For example, in the next code snippet, we declare three variables, **v1**, **v2**, and **v3** in one statement. This is because they are of the same type (i.e., **integers**).

```
int v1,v2,v3;
int v4=4, v5=5, v6=6;
```

In the code above, the first line declares the variables v1, v2, and v3. All three are integers. In the second line, not only do we declare three variables simultaneously, but we also initialize them (i.e., set a value).

When using variables, there are a few things that we need to determine including their name, type and scope:

- **Name of a variable:** A variable is usually given a unique name so that it can be identified uniquely. The name of a variable is usually referred to as an identifier. When defining an identifier, it can contain letters, digits, a minus, an underscore or a dollar sign, and it usually begins with a letter. Identifiers cannot be keywords (e.g., such as **if**).

- **Type of variable:** variables can hold several types of data including numbers (e.g., **integers, doubles** or **floats**), text (i.e., strings or characters), Boolean values (e.g., true or false), arrays, objects (i.e., we will see this concept later in this chapter) or **GameObjects** (i.e., any object included in your scene), as illustrated in the next code snippet.

```
string myName = "Patrick";//the text is declared using double quotes
int currentYear = 2015;//the year needs no decimals and is declared as an integer
float width = 100.45f;//width is declared as a float (i.e., with decimals)
```

- **Variable declaration:** a variable needs to be declared so that the system knows what you referring to if you use it in your code. To create a variable, it needs to be declared. At the declaration stage, the variable does not have to be assigned a value, and this can be done later.

```
string myName;
myName = "My Name"
```

In the previous example, we declare a variable called **myName** and then assign the value **"My Name"** to it.

- **Scope of a variable:** a variable can be accessed (i.e., referred to) in specific contexts that depend on where in the script the variable was declared. We will look at this principle later.

- **Accessibility level:** as we will see later, a C# programme consists of classes; for each of these classes, the methods and variables within can be accessed depending on **accessibility** levels. We will look at this principle later on (there is no need for any confusion at this stage :-)).

Common variable types include:

- **String**: same as text.

- **Int**: integer (1, 2, 3, etc.).

- **Boolean**: true or false.

- **Float**: with a fractional value (e.g., 1.2f, 3.4f, etc.).

- **Arrays**: a group of variables of the same type. If this is unclear, not to worry, this concept will be explained further in this chapter.

- **GameObject**: a game object (any game object in your scene).

ARRAYS

Sometimes, to make your code leaner, arrays make it easier to apply features and similar behaviors to a wide range of data. Arrays can help to declare less variables (for variables storing the same type of information) and to also access them more easily. When creating arrays, you can create single-dimensional arrays and multidimensional arrays.

Let's look at the simplest form of arrays: single-dimensional arrays. For this concept, we can take the analogy of a group of 10 people who all have a name. If we wanted to store this information using a string variable, we would need to declare (and set) ten different variables.

```
string name1;string name2; ......
```

While this code is perfectly fine, it would be great to store these in only one variable. For this purpose, we could use an array. An array is comparable to a list of elements that we access using an index. This index usually starts at 0 (for the first element in the list).

So let's see how we could do this with an array; first we could declare the array as follows:

```
string [] names;
```

You will probably notice the syntax **dataType [] nameofTheArray**. The **[]** syntax means that we declare an **array** of string values.

Then we could initialize the array, as we would normally do with any variable:

```
names = new string [10];
```

In the previous code, we just say that our new array called **names** will include 10 string variables.

We can then store information in this array as described in the next code snippet.

```
names [0] = "Paul";
names [1] = "Mary";
...
names [9] = "Pat";
```

In the previous code, we store the name **Paul** as the first element in the array (remember the index starts at 0); we store the second element (with the index 1) as **Mary**, as well as the last element (index is 9), **Pat**.

> Note that for an array of size **n, the index of the first element is 0** and **the index of the last element is n-1**. So for an array of size 10, the index for the first element is 0, and the index of the last element is 9.

If you were to use arrays of integers or floats, or any other type of data, the process would be similar.

Now, one of the cool things you can do with arrays is that you can initialize your array in one line, saving you the headaches of writing 10 lines of code if you have 10 variables, as illustrated in the next example.

```
string [] names = new string [10] {"Paul","Mary","John","Mark",
"Eva","Pat","Sinead","Elma","Flaithri", "Eleanor"};
```

This is very handy, as you will see in the next chapters, and this should definitely save you time coding.

Now that we have looked into single-dimensional arrays, let's look at multidimensional arrays, which can also be very handy when storing information. This type of array (i.e., multidimensional array) can be compared to a building with several floors, and on each floor, several apartments. So let's say that we would like to store the number of tenants for each apartment; we would, in this case, create variables that would store this number for each of these apartments.

The first solution would be to create variables that store the number of tenants for each of these apartments with a variable that makes reference to the floor, and the number of the apartment. For example **ap0_1** could be for the first apartment on the ground floor, **ap0_2**, would then be for the second apartment on the ground floor, **ap1_1**, would then be for the first apartment on the first floor, and **ap1_2**, would then be for the second apartment on the first floor. So in term of coding, we could have the following:

```
int ap0_1 = 0;
int ap0_2 = 0;
...
```

Using arrays instead we could do the following:

```
int [,] apArray = new int [10,10];
apArray [0,1] = 0;
apArray [0,2] = 0;
print (apArray[0]);
```

In the previous code:

- We declare our array. **int [,]** means an array that has two dimensions; in other words, we say that any element in this array will be defined and accessed based on two parameters: the floor level and the number of this apartment on that level.

Introduction to Programming *in C#*

- We also specify a size (or maximum) for each of these parameters. The maximum number of floors (level) will be 10, and the maximum number of apartment per floor will be 10. So, for this example we can define levels, from level 0 to level 9 (that would be 10 levels), and from apartment 0 to apartment 9 (that would be 10 apartment).

- The last line of code prints (in the **Console** window) the value of the first element of the array.

> One of the other interesting things with arrays is that, using a loop, you can write a single line of code to access all the elements of this array, and hence, write more efficient code.

CONSTANTS

So far we have looked at variables and how you can store and access them seamlessly. The assumption then was that a value may change over time, and that this value would be stored in a variable. However, there may be times when you know that a value will remain constant. For example, you may want to define labels that refer to values that should not change over time, and in this case, you could use constants. Let me explain: let's say that the player may have three choices in the game (e.g., referred to as 0, 1, and 2) and that you don't really want to remember these values, or that you would like to use a way that makes it easier to refer to them. Let's look at the following code:

```
int userChoice = 2;
if (userChoice == 0) print ("you have decided to restart");
if (userChoice == 1) print ("you have decided to stop the game");
if (userChoice == 2) print ("you have decided to pause the game");
```

In the previous code:

- The variable **userChoice** is an integer and is set to 1.

- Then we check its value and print a message accordingly.

Now, you may or may not remember that 0 corresponds to restarting the game; the same applies to the other two values. So instead, we could use constants to make it easier to remember (and use) these values. Let's look at the equivalent code that uses constants.

```
const int CHOICE_RESTART = 0;
const int CHOICE_STOP = 1;
const int CHOICE_PAUSE = 2;
int userChoice = 2;
if (userChoice == CHOICE_RESTART) print ("you have decided to restart");
if (userChoice == CHOICE_STOP) print ("you have decided to stop the game");
if (userChoice == CHOICE_PAUSE) print ("you have decided to pause the game");
```

In the previous code:

- We declare three **constant** variables.

- These variables are then used to check the choice made by the user.

In the next example, we use a constant to calculate a tax rate; this is a good practice as the same value will be used across the programme with no or little room for errors when it comes to using the exact same tax rate across the code.

Introduction to Programming in C#

```
const float VAT_RATE = 0.21f;
float priceBeforeVat = 23.0f
float priceAfterVat = pricebeforeVat * VAT_RATE;
```

In the previous code:

- We declare a **constant** float variable for the vat rate.

- We declare a **float** variable for the item's price before the vat.

- We calculate the item's price after adding tax.

> It is a very good coding practice to use constants for values that don't change across your programmme. Using constants makes your code more readable; it saves work when you need to change a value in your code, and it also decreases possible occurrences of errors (e.g., for calculations).

OPERATORS

Once we have declared and assigned values to a variable, we can use operators to modify or combine variables. There are different types of operators including: arithmetic operators, assignment operators, comparison operators and logical operators.

Arithmetic operators are used to perform arithmetic operations including additions, subtractions, multiplications, or divisions. Common arithmetic operators include +, -, *, /, or % (modulo).

```
int number1 = 1;// the variable number1 is declared
int number2 = 1;// the variable number2 is declared
int sum = number1 + number2;// adding two numbers and store them in sum
int sub = number1 - number2;// subtracting two numbers and store them in sub
```

Assignment operators can be used to assign a value to a variable and include =, +=, -=, *=, /= or %=.

```
int number1 = 1;
int number2 = 1;
number1+=1; //same as number1 = number1 + 1;
number1-=1; //same as number1 = number1 - 1;
number1*=1; //same as number1 = number1 * 1;
number1/=1; //same as number1 = number1 / 1;
number1%=1; //same as number1 = number1 % 1;
```

Note that the = operator, when used with strings, will concatenate strings (i.e., add them one after the other to create a new string). When used with a number and a string, the same will apply (for example **"Hello"+1** will result in **"Hello1"**).

Comparison operators are often used for conditions to compare two values; comparison operators include ==, !=, >, <, >= and >=.

```
if (number1 == number2); //if number1 equals number2
if (number1 != number2); //if number1 and number2 have different values
if (number1 > number2); //if number1 is greater than number2
if (number1 >= number2); //if number1 is greater than or equal to number2
if (number1 < number2); //if number1 is less than number2
if (number1 <= number2); //if number1 is less than or equal to number2
```

CONDITIONAL STATEMENTS

Statements can be performed based on a condition, and in this case they are called **conditional statements**. The syntax is usually as follows:

```
If (condition) statement;
```

This means **if the condition is verified (or true) then (and only then) the statement is executed**. When we assess a condition, we test whether a declaration is true. For example by typing if (a == b), we mean "**if it is true that a equals to b**". Similarly, if we type **if (a>=b)** we mean "**if its is true that a is greater than or equal to b**"

As we will see later on, we can also combine conditions. For example, we can decide to perform a statement if two (or more) conditions are true. For example, by typing **if (a == b && c == 2)** we mean "**if a equals to b and c equals to 2**". In this case using the operator **&&** means **AND**, and that both conditions will need to be true. We could compare this to making a decision on whether we will go sailing tomorrow. For example "**if the weather is sunny and the wind speed is less than 5km/h then I will go sailing**". We could translate this statement as follows.

```
if (weatherIsSunny == true && windSpeed < 5) IGoSailing = true;
```

When creating conditions, as for most natural languages, we can use the operator **OR** noted ||. Taking the previous example, we could translate the following sentence "**if the weather is too hot or the wind is faster than 5km/h then I will not go sailing** " as follows.

```
if (weatherIsTooHot == true || windSpeed >5) IGoSailing = false;
```

Another example could be as follows.

```
if (myName == "Patrick") print("Hello Patrick");
else print ("Hello Stranger");
```

> When we deal with combining true or false statements, we are effectively applying what is called **Boolean logic**. Boolean logic deals with Boolean variables that have two values 1 and 0 (or true and false). By evaluating conditions, we are effectively processing Boolean numbers and applying Boolean logic. While you don't need to know about Boolean logic in depth, some operators for Boolean logic are important, including the ! operator. It means **NOT** or the opposite. This means that if a variable is true, its opposite will be false, and vice versa. For example, if we consider the variable **weatherIsGood = true**, the value of **!weatherIsGood** will be **false** (its opposite). So the condition **if (weatherIdGood == false)** could be also written **if (!weatherIsGood)** which would literally translate as "if the weather is **NOT** good".

SWITCH STATEMENTS

If you have understood the concept of conditional statements, then this section should be pretty much straight forward. Switch statements are a variation on the if/else statements that we have seen earlier. The idea behind the switch statement is that, depending on the value of a particular variable, we will switch to a particular portion of the code and perform one or several actions. The variable considered for the switch structure is usually of type **integer**. Let's look at a simple example:

```
int choice = 1;
switch (choice)
{
      case 1:
            print ("you chose 1");
            break;
      case 2:
            print ("you chose 2");
            break;
      case 3:
            print ("you chose 3");
            break;
      default:
            print ("Default option");
            break;
}
print ("We have exited the switch structure");
```

In the previous code:

- We declare the variable **choice**, as an **integer** and initialize it to **1**.

- We then create a **switch** structure whereby, depending on the value of the variable **choice**, the programme will switch to the relevant section (i.e., the portion of code starting with **case 1:**, **case 2:**, etc.). Note that in our code, we look for the values 1, 2 or 3. However, if the variable **choice** does not equal 1 or 2 or 3, the program will branch to the section called **default**. This is because this section is executed if any of the other possible choices (i.e., 1,2, or 3) have not been fulfilled (or selected).

Introduction to Programming in C#

> Note that each choice or branch starts with the keyword **case** and ends with **break**. The **break** statement is there to specify that after executing the commands included in the branch (or current choice), it should exit the switch structure. Without any break statement the next line of code will be executed.

So let's consider the previous example and see how this would work. In our case, the variable **choice** is set to **1**, so we will enter the **switch** structure, and then look for the section that deals with a value of **1** for the variable **choice**. This will be the section that starts with **case 1:**; then the command **print ("you chose 1");** will be executed, followed by the command **break**, indicating that we should exit the switch structure; finally the command **print ("We have exited the switch structure")** will be executed.

> Switch structures are very useful to structure your code and when dealing with mutually exclusive choices (i.e., only one of the choices can be processed) based on an integer value, especially in the case of menus. In addition switch structures make for cleaner and easily understandable code.

LOOPS

There are times when you have to perform repetitive tasks as a programmer; many times, these can be fast forwarded using loops. Loops are structures that will perform the same actions repetitively based on a condition. So, the process is usually as follows:

- Start the loop.
- Perform actions.
- Check for a condition.
- Exit the loop if the condition is fulfilled or keep looping.

Sometimes the condition is performed at the start of the loop, some other times it is performed at the end of the loop.

Let's take the following example that is using a **while** loop.

```
int counter =0;
while (counter <=10)
{
        print ("Counter = " + counter);
        counter++;
}
```

In the previous code:

- We set the value of the variable **counter**.
- We then create a loop that is delimited by the curly brackets and that starts with the keyword **while**.
- We set the condition to remain in this loop (i.e., **counter <=10**).
- Within the loop, we increase the value of the variable **counter** by 1 and print its value.

So effectively:

- The first time we go through the loop: the variable **counter** is increased to **1**; we reach the end of the loop; we go back to the start of the loop and check if **counter** is <=10; this is true in this case (**counter** = 1).
- The second time we go through the loop: **counter** is increased to 2; we reach the end of the loop; we go back to the start of the loop and check if **counter** is <=10; this is true in this case (**counter** = 2).

Introduction to Programming in C#

- ...
  - The 11th time we go through the loop: **counter** is increased to 11; we reach the end of the loop; we go back to the start and check if **counter** is <=10; this is now false in this case (**counter** = 11). As a result, we then exit the loop.

So, as you can see, using a loop, we have managed to increment the value of the variable **counter** iteratively, from 0 to 11, but using less code than would be needed otherwise.

Now, we could create a slightly modified version of this loop; let's look at the following example:

```
int counter =0;
do
{
        print ("Counter = " + counter);
        counter++;
} while (counter <=10);
```

In this example, you may spot two differences, compared to the previous code:

- The **while** keyword is now at the end of the loop. So the condition will be evaluated (or assessed) at the end of the loop.
- A **do** keyword is now featured at the start of the loop.
- In this example, we perform statements and then check for the condition.

Another variations of the code could be as follows:

```
for (int counter = 0; counter <=10; counter ++)
{
        print ("Counter = " + counter);
}
```

In the previous code:

- We declare a loop in a slight different way: we say that we will use an integer variable called **counter** that will go from 0 to 10.
- This variable **counter** will be incremented by 1 every time we go through the loop.
- We remain in the loop as long as the variable **counter** is less than or equal to 10.
- The test for the condition, in this case, is performed at the start of the loop.

Loops are very useful to be able to perform repetitive actions for a finite number of objects, or to perform what is usually referred as recursive actions. For example, you could use loops to create (i.e., instantiate) 100 objects at different locations (this will save you some code :-)), or to go through an array of 100+ elements.

CLASSES

When coding in C# with Unity, you will be creating scripts that are either classes or use built-in classes. So what is a class?

As we have seen earlier, C# is an object-oriented programming (OOP) language. Put simply, a C# programme will consist of a collection of objects that interact amongst themselves. Each object has one or more attributes, and it is possible to perform actions on these objects using what are called **methods**. In addition, objects that share the same properties are said to belong to the same **class**. For example, we could take the analogy of a bike. There are bikes of all shapes and colors; however, they share common features. For example, they all have a specific number of wheels (e.g., one, two or three) or a speed; they can have a color, and actions can be performed on these bikes (e.g., accelerate, turn right, turn left, etc.). So in object-oriented programming, the class would be **bike**, speed or color would be referred as member variables, and accelerate (i.e., an action) would be referred as member methods. So if we were to define a common type, we could define a class called **Bike** and for this class define several member variables and attributes that would make it possible to define and perform actions on the objects of type **Bike**.

This is, obviously, a simplified explanation of classes and objects, but it should give you a clearer idea of the concept of object-oriented programming, if you are new to it.

DEFINING A CLASS

So now that we have a clearer idea of what a class is, let's see how we could define a class. So let's look at the following example.

```
public class Bike
{
      private float speed;
      private int color;

      public void accelerate()
      {
            speed++;
      }
      public void turnRight()
      {
      }
      private void calculateDistance()
      {
      }
}
```

In the code above, we have defined a class, called **Bike**, that includes two member variables (**speed** and **color**) as well as two member methods (**accelerate** and **turnRight**). Let's look at the script a little closer; you may notice a few things:

- The name of the class is preceded by the keywords **public class**; in OOP terms, the keyword **public** is called an **access modifier** and it defines how (and from where) this class may be accessed and used. In C# there are at least five types of access modifiers, including **public** (no restricted access), **protected** (access limited to the containing class or types derived from this class), **internal** (access is limited to the current assembly), **protected internal** (we won't be using this access mode in this book), and **private** (access only from the containing type).

- The names of all variables are preceded by their type (i.e., int), and the keyword **private**: this means that these integer variables will be accessible only within this class.

- Some of the names of the methods are preceded by the keywords **public void** (e.g., for the methods **accelerate** or **turnRight**): the **void** keyword means that the method does not return any data back, while the keyword **public** means that the method will be accessible throughout our programme.

- Some of the names of the methods are preceded by the keywords **private void** (e.g., for the method **calculateDistance**): the **void** keyword means that the method does not return

[25]

any data back, while the keyword **private** means that the method will be accessible only from the containing type (i.e., **Bike**).

ACCESSING CLASS MEMBERS AND VARIABLES

Once a class has been defined, it's great to be able to access its member variables and methods. In C# (as for other object-oriented programming languages), this can be done using the **dot notation**.

> The dot notation refers to **object-oriented programming**. Using dots, you can access properties and functions (or methods) related to a particular object. For example **gameObject.transform.position** gives you access to the **position** from the **transform** of the object linked to this script. It is often useful to read it backward; in this case, the dot can be interpreted as **"of"**. So in our case, **gameObject.transform.position** can be translated as "the position **of** the transform **of** the **gameObject**".

Once a class has been defined, objects based on this class can be created. For example, if we were to create a new **Bike** object, based on the code that we have seen above, the following code could be used.

```
Bike myBike = new Bike();
```

This code will create an object based on the "template" **Bike**. You may notice the syntax:

```
dataType variable = new dataType()
```

By default, this new object will include all the member variables and methods defined earlier. So it will have a color and a speed, and we should also be able to access its **accelerate** and **turnRight** methods. So how can this be done? Let's look at the next code snippet that shows how we can access these.

```
Bike b = new Bike();
b.accelerate();
```

In the previous code:

- The new bike **myBike** is created.

- The speed is then increased after calling the **accelerate** method. This method can be called using the dot notation because it is **public**.

- Note that to call an object's method we use the dot notation.

Introduction to Programming in C#

> When defining member variables and methods, it is usually good practice to restrict the access to member variables (e.g., private type) and to define public methods with no or less strict restrictions (e.g., public) that provide access to these variables. These methods are often referred to as **getters** and **setters** (because you can get or set values from them).

To illustrate this concept, let's look at the following code:

```
public class Bike
{
    private float speed;
    private int color;
    public void accelerate()
    {
        speed++;
    }
    public void turnRight()
    {
    }
    private void claculateDistance()
    {

    }
    public void setSpeed(float newSpeed)
    {
        speed = newSpeed;
    }
    public float getSpeed()
    {
        return (speed)
    }
}
```

In the previous code, we have declared two new methods: **setSpeed** and **getSpeed**.

- For **setSpeed**: the type is **void** as this method does not return any information, and its access is set to **public**, so that it can be accessed with no restrictions.

- For **getSpeed**: the type is **float** as this method returns the speed, which type is float. Its access is set to **public**, so that it can be accessed with no restrictions.

So, we could combine the code created to date in one programme (or new class) as follows in Unity.

Introduction to Programming in C#

```
using UnityEngine;
using System.Collections;

public class TestCode : MonoBehaviour {
    public class Bike
    {
        private float speed;
        private int color;
        public void accelerate()
        {
            speed++;
        }
        public void turnRight()
        {
        }
        private void claculateDistance()
        {


        }
        public void setSpeed(float newSpeed)
        {
            speed = newSpeed;
        }
        public float getSpeed()
        {
            return (speed)
        }

    }
    public void Start ()
    {
        Bike myBike = new Bike();
        myBike.setSpeed (23.0f);
        print (myBike.getSpeed());
    }
}
```

In the previous code, you may notice at least two differences compared to the previous code that we have created:

- At the start of the code, the following two lines of code have been added:

```
using UnityEngine;
using System.Collections;
```

- The keyword **using** is called a directive; in this particular case it is used to import what is called a **namespace**; put simply, by adding this directive you are effectively importing (or

Introduction to Programming in C#

gaining access to) a collection of classes or data types. Each of these namespaces or "libraries" includes useful classes for your programme. For example, the namespace **UnityEngine** will include classes for Unity development and **System.Collections** will include classes and interfaces for different collections of objects. By default, whenever you create a new C# script in Unity, these two namespaces (and associated directives) are included.

- We have declared our class **Bike** within another class called **TestCode**. **TestCode** is, in this case, the containing class.

```
public class TestCode : MonoBehaviour {
```

- Whenever you create a new C# script, the name of the script (for example **TestCode** will be used to define the main class within the script; i.e., **TestCode**).

- The **syntax: Monobehavior** means that the class **TestCode** is derived from the class **MonoBehaviour**. This is often referred to as inheritance.

CONSTRUCTORS

As we have seen in the previous section, when a new object is created, it will, by default, include all the member variables and methods. To create this object, we would use the name of the class, followed by (), as per the next example.

```
Bike myBike = new Bike();
myBike.accelerate();
```

In fact, it is possible to change some of the properties of the new object created at the time it is initialized. For example, instead of setting the speed and the color of the object as we have done in the previous code, it would be great to be able to set these automatically and pass the parameter accordingly when the object is created. Well, this can be done with what is called a **constructor**. A constructor literally helps to construct your new object based on parameters (also referred as arguments) and instructions. So, for example, let's say that we would like the color of our bike to be specified when it is created; we could modify the **Bike** class, as follows, by adding the following method:

```
public Bike (int newColor)
{
    color = newColor;
}
```

This is a new constructor (the name of the method is the same as the class), and it takes an integer as a parameter; so after modifying the description of our class (as per the code above), we could then create a new bike object as follows:

```
Bike myBike = new Bike(2);
```

We could even specify a second constructor that would include both the color and the speed as follows:

```
public Bike (int newColor, float newSpeed)
{
    color = newColor;
    speed = newSpeed;
}
```

You can have different constructors in your class; the constructor used at the initialization stage will be the one that matches the arguments passed.

For example, let's say that we have two constructors for our Bike class.

```
public Bike (int newColor)
{
        color = newColor;
}

public Bike (int newColor, float newSpeed)
{
        color = newColor;
        speed = newSpeed;
}
```

If a new **Bike** object is created as follows:

```
Bike newBike = new Bike (2)
```

...then the first constructor will be called.

If a new **Bike** object is created as follows:

```
Bike newBike = new Bike (2, 10.0f)
```

...then the second constructor will be called.

You may also wonder what happens if the following code is used since no default constructor has been defined.

```
Bike newBike = new Bike ();
```

In fact, whenever you create your class, a default constructor is also defined (implicitly) and evoked whenever a new object is created using the **new** operator with no arguments. This is called a default constructor. In this case, the default values for each of the types of the numerical member variables are used (e.g., 0 for integers or false for Boolean variables).

Note that access to constructors is usually public, except in the particular cases where we would like a class not to be instantiated (e.g., for classes that include **static** members only). Also note that, as for variables, if no access modifiers are specified, these will be **private** by default. This is similar for methods.

DESTRUCTORS

As for constructors, when an object is deleted, the corresponding destructor is called. Its name is the same as the class and preceded by a tilde ~; as illustrated in the next code snippet.

```
~Bike()
{
     //add some code here;
}
```

This being said, a destructor can neither take parameters (or arguments) nor return a value.

STATIC MEMBERS OF A CLASS

When a method or variable is declared as static, only one instance of this member exists for a class. So a static variable will be "shared" between instances of this class. Static variables are usually used to retrieve constants without instantiating a class. The same applies for static method: they can be evoked without having to instantiate a class. This can be very useful if you want to create and avail of tools. For example, in Unity, it is possible to use the method **GameObject.Find**(); this method usually makes it possible to look for a particular object based on its name. Let's look at the following example.

```
public void Start()
{
    GameObject t = (GameObject) GameObject.Find("test");
}
```

In the previous code, we look for an object called test, and store the result inside the variable **t** of type **GameObject**. However, when we use the syntax **GameObject.Find**, we use the static method **Find** that is available from the class **GameObject**. There are many other static functions that you will be able to use in Unity, including **Instantiate**. Again, these functions can be called without the need to instantiate an object. The following code snippet provides another example based on the class **Bike**.

```
using UnityEngine;
using System.Collections;

public class TestCode : MonoBehaviour {

    public class Bike
    {
        private float speed;
        private int color;
        private float speed;
        private int color;
        private static int nbBikes;
        public void countBikes()
        {
            nbBikes++;
        }
        public int getNbBikes()
        {
            return (nbBikes);
        }
    }
    void Start ()
    {
        Bike bike1 = new Bike();
        Bike bike2 = new Bike();
        bike1.countBikes();
        bike2.countBikes();
        print("Nb Bikes:"+bike1.getNbBikes());

    }}
```

The following code illustrates the use of static functions.

```
using UnityEngine;
using System.Collections;
public class TestCode : MonoBehaviour
{
    public class Bike
    {
        private float speed;
        private int color;
        public static void sayHello()
        {
            print("Hello");
        }
    }
    public void Start()
    {
        Bike.sayHello();
    }
}
```

The previous code would result in the following output:

```
Hello
```

In the previous code, we declare a static method called **sayHello**; this method is then called in the start method without the need to instantiate (or create) a new **Bike**. This is because, due to its **public** and **static** attributes, it can be accessed from anywhere in the programme.

INHERITANCE

I hope everything is clear so far, as we are going to look at a very interesting and important principle for object-oriented programming: inheritance. The main idea of inheritance is that objects can inherit their properties from other objects (their parent). As they inherit these properties, they can remain identical or evolve and overwrite some of these inherited properties. This is very interesting because it makes it possible to minimize the code by creating a class with general properties for all objects sharing similar features, and then, if need be, to overwrite and customize some of these properties.

Let's take the example of vehicles; they would generally have the following properties:

- Number of wheels.
- Speed.
- Number of passengers.
- Color.
- Capacity to accelerate.
- Capacity to stop.

So we could create the following class for example:

```
class Vehicles
{
    private int nbWheels;
    protected float speed;
    private int nbPassengers;
    private int color;
    public void accelerate()
    {
        speed++;
    }
}
```

These features could apply for example to cars, bikes, motorbikes, or trucks. However, all these vehicles also differ; some of them may or may not have an engine or a steering wheel. So we could create a subclass called **MotorizedVehicles**, based on **Vehicles**, but with specificities linked to the fact that they are motorized. These added attributes could be:

- Engine size.
- Petrol type.

Introduction to Programming in C#

- Petrol levels.
- Ability to fill-up the tank.

The following example illustrates how this class could be created.

```
class MotoredVehicles: Vehicles
{
        private float engineSize;
        private int petrolType;
        private float petrolLevels;
        public void fillUpTank()
        {
                petrolLevels+=10;
        }
}
```

- When the class is defined, its name is followed by: **Vehicles**. This means that it inherits from the class **Vehicles**. So it will, by default, avail of all the methods and variables already included in the class **Vehicles**.

- We have created a new member method for this class, called **fillUpTank**.

- In the previous example, you may notice that the methods and variables that were defined for the class **Vehicles** do not appear here; this is because they are implicitly added to this new class, since it inherits from the class **Vehicles**.

Whenever you create a new class in Unity, it will, by default, inherit from the **MonoBehaviour** class; as a result, it will implicitly include all the member methods and variables of the class **MonoBehaviour**. Some of these methods include **Start** or **Update**, for example.

> When using inheritance, the parent is usually referred to as the **base class**, while the child is referred to as the **inherited class**.

Now, while the child inherits "Behaviors" from its parents, these can always be modified or, put simply, overwritten. However, in this case, the base method (the method defined in the parent) must be declared as virtual. Also, when overriding this method, the keyword **override** must be used. This is illustrated in the following code.

```
class Vehicles
{
    private int nbWheels;
    protected float speed;
    private int nbPassengers;
    private int color;
    public virtual void accelerate()
    {
        speed++;
    }
}
class MotoredVehicles : Vehicles
{
    private float engineSize;
    private int petrolType;
    private float petrolLevels;
    private void fillUpTank()
    {
        petrolLevels += 10;
    }
    public override void accelerate()
    {
        speed += 10;
    }
}
```

In the previous example, while the method **accelerate** is inherited from the class **Vehicles**, it would normally increase the speed by one. However, by overwriting it, we make sure that in the case of objects instantiated from the class **MotoredVehicles**, each acceleration increases the speed by 10. We can access the member variable speed from the child class **MotoredVehicles** because it has been declared as **protected**.

This point can also be illustrated using some classes in Unity. Let's look at the next example.

```
using UnityEngine;
using System.Collections;

public class TestCode : MonoBehaviour {

    public class Bike
    {
        private float speed;
        private int color;
        public static void sayHello()
        {
            print ("Hello");
        }
    }
    public void Start ()
    {
        Bike.sayHello();
    }
}
```

In this example, we have created a class **TestCode**; this class inherits from **MonoBehaviour**; by default this class includes, amongst other things, a definition for the methods **Start** and **Update**; however, by default, these two methods are blank; this is the reason why we overwrite these methods for the class **TestCode** (inherited from **MonoBehaviour**) so that the **Start** method actually displays some information.

There are obviously more concepts linked to inheritance; however, the information provided in this section should get you started easily. For more information on inheritance in C#, you can look at the official documentation.

METHODS

Methods or functions can be compared to a friend or colleague to whom you gently ask to perform a task, based on specific instructions, and to return the information to you then. For example, you could ask your friend the following: "**Can you please tell me when I will be celebrating my 20th birthday given that I was born in 2000**". So you give your friend (who is good at Math :-)) the information (date of birth) and s/he will calculate the year of your 20th birthday and give this information back to you. So in other words, your friend will be given an input (i.e., the date of birth) and return an output (i.e., the year of your 20th birthday). Methods work exactly this way: they are given information (and sometimes not), perform an action, and then (sometimes, if needed) return information back.

In programming terms, a method (or function) is a block of instructions that performs a set of actions. It is executed when invoked (or put more simply **called**) from the script, or when an event occurs (e.g., the player has clicked on a button or the player collides with an object; we will see more about events in the next section). As for member variables, member functions or methods are declared and they can also be called.

Methods are very useful because once the code for a method has been created, it can be called several times without the need to re-write the same code over and over again. Also, because methods can take parameters, a method can process these parameters and produce or return information accordingly; in other words, they can perform different actions and produce different information based on the input. As a result, methods can do one or all of the following:

- Perform an action.

- Return a result.

- Take parameters and process them.

A method has a syntax and can be declared as follows (in at least two ways).

```
AccessType typeOfdataReturned nameOfTheFunction ()
{
        Perform actions here…
}
```

In the previous code the method does not take any input; neither does it return an output. It just performs actions.

OR

Introduction to Programming in C#

```
AccessType typeOfDataReturned nameOfTheFunction ()
{
        Perform actions here…
}
```

Let's look at the following method for instance.

```
public int calculateSum(int a, int b)
{
        return (a+b);
}
```

In the previous code:

- The method is of type **public**: there are no access restrictions.

- The method will return an integer.

- The name of the method is **calculateSum**.

- The method takes two arguments (i.e., integer parameters).

- The method returns the sum of the two parameters passed (the parameters are referred to as **a** and **b** within this method).

A method can be called using the **()** operator, as follows:

```
nameOfTheFunction1();
nameOfTheFunction2(value);
int test = nameOfTheFunction3(value);
```

In the previous code, a method is called with no parameter (line 1), or with a parameter (line 2). In the third example (line 3), a variable called **test** will be set with the value returned by the method **nameOfTheFunction3**.

> You may, and we will get to this later, have different methods in a class with the exact same name but that take different types of parameters. This is often referred as polymorphism, as the method literally takes different forms and can process information differently based on the information (e.g., type of data) provided.

ACCESSING METHODS AND ACCESS MODIFIERS

As we have seen previously, in C# there are different types of access modifiers. These modifiers specify from where a method can be called and can be **public** (no restricted access), **protected** (access is limited to the containing class or types derived from this class), **internal** (access is limited to the current assembly), **protected internal** (we won't use this access type in this book), and **private** (i.e., access is limited to the containing type).

COMMON METHODS

In Unity, there are many methods available by default, and they are called built-in methods. Some of these functions are called when an event occurs. For example:

- **Start**: called at the start of the scene.

- **Update**: called every time the screen is refreshed.

- **OnControllerColliderHit**: called whenever the **First-Person Controller** (a built-in controller used to make it possible to navigate through your scene using a first-person view) collides with an object.

As we will see later, because most of your classes will inherit by default from the class **MonoBehaviour**, they will, by default, include several methods, including **Start** and **Update** that you will be able to override (i.e., modify for your own use).

SCOPE OF VARIABLES

Whenever you create a variable in C#, you will need to be aware of the scope and access type of the variable so that you use it where its scope makes it possible for you to do so.

The scope of a variable refers to where you can use this variable in a script. In C#, we usually make the difference between **global variables** and **local variables**.

> You can compare the term **local** and **global** variables to a language that is either local or global. In the first case, the local language will only be used (i.e., spoken) by the locals, whereas the global language will be used (i.e., spoken) and understood by anyone whether they are locals or part of the global community.

When you create a class definition along with member variables, these variables will be seen by any method within your class.

Global variables are variables that can be used anywhere in your script, hence the name global. These variables need to be declared at the start of the script (using the usual declaration syntax) and outside of any method; they can then be used anywhere in the script as illustrated in the next code snippet.

```
class MyBike
{
        private int color;
        private float speed;

        public void accelerate()
        {
                speed++;
        }
}
```

In the previous code we declare the variable **speed** as a member variable and access it from the method accelerate.

Local variables are declared within a method and are to be used only within this method, hence the term local, because they can only be used locally, as illustrated in the next code snippet.

```
public void Start()
{
    int myVar;
    myVar = 0;
}
public void Update()
{
    int myVar2;
    myVar2 = 2;
}
```

In the previous code, **myVar** is a local variable to the method **Start**, and can only be used within this function; **myVar2** is a local variable to the method **Update**, and can only be used within this method.

EVENTS

Throughout this book and in C#, you will read about and use events. So what are they?

Well, put simply, events can be compared to something that happens at a particular time, and when this event occurs, something (e.g., an action) needs to be done. If we make an analogy with daily activities: when the alarm goes off (event) we can either get-up (action) or decide to go back to sleep. When you receive an email (event), you can decide to read it (action), and then reply to the sender (another action).

In computer terms, it is quite similar, although the events that we will be dealing with will be slightly different. So, we could be waiting for the user to press a key (event) and then move the character accordingly (action), or wait until the user clicks on a button on screen (event) to load a new scene (action).

In Unity, whenever an event occurs, a function (or method) is usually called (the function, in this case, is often referred as a handler, because it "handles" the event). You have then the opportunity to modify this function and add instructions (i.e. statements) that should be followed, should this event occur.

> To take the analogy of daily activities: we could write instructions to a friend on a piece of paper, so that, in case someone calls in our absence, the friend knows exactly what to do. So an event handler is basically a set of instructions (usually stored within a function) to be followed in case a particular event occurs.

Sometimes information is passed to this method about the particular event, and sometimes not. For example, when the screen is refreshed the method **Update** is called. When the game starts (i.e., when a particular script is enabled), the method **Start** is called. When there is a collision between the player and an object, the method **OnControllerColliderHit** is called. In this particular case (i.e., collision), an object is usually passed to the method that handles the event so that we get to know more about the other object involved in the collision.

As you can see, there can be a wide range of events in our game, and we will get to that later on. In this book, we will essentially be dealing with the following events:

- **Start**: when a script is enabled (e.g., start of the scene).

- **Update**: when the screen is refreshed (e.g., every frame).

- **OnControllerColliderHit**: when a collision occurs between the player and another object.

- **Awake**: when the game starts (i.e., once).

POLYMORPHISM (GENERAL CONCEPTS)

The word polymorphism takes its meaning from **poly** (several) and **morph** (shape); so it literally means several forms. In object-oriented programming, it refers to the ability to process objects differently (or more specifically) depending on their data type or class. Let's take the example of adding. If we want to add two numbers, we will make an algebraic addition (e.g., 1 + 2). However, adding two **string** variables may mean concatenating them (adding them one after the other). For example, adding the text "Hello" and the text "World" would result in the text "**HelloWorld**". As you can see, the way an operation is performed on different data types may vary and produce different results. So again, with polymorphism we will be able to customize methods (or operations) so that data is processed based on its type of class. So, let's look at the following code which illustrates how this can be done in C#.

```
public class AddObjects
{
    public int add (int a, int b)
    {
        return (a + b);
    }
    public string add (string a, string b)
    {
        return (a + b);
    }
}
```

In the previous code, it is possible to add two different types of data: integers and strings. Depending on whether two integers or two strings are passed as parameters, we will be calling either the first **add** method or the second **add** method.

DYNAMIC POLYMORPHISM

In C#, dynamic polymorphism can be achieved using both abstract classes and virtual functions.

In C#, it is possible to create a class that will provide a partial implementation of an interface. Broadly, an interface defines what a class should include (i.e., member methods, member variables or events), but it does not declare how these should be implemented. So, an abstract class will include abstract methods or variables; which means that this class will define the name and type of the variables, the name of the methods, as well as the type of data returned by this method. It is called **abstract** because you cannot implement this type of class (it can never be "materialized"); however, it can be used as a template (or "dream" class) for derived classes. Let's look at the following example.

```
abstract class Vehicule
{
    public abstract void decelerate();
}

class Bike : Vehicule
{
    private float speed;
    private int color;
    public Bike(float newSpeed)
    {
        speed = newSpeed;
    }
    public override void decelerate()
    {
        speed--;
    }
}
```

In the previous code:

- We declare an abstract class **Vehicle**.

- We declare an abstract method called **decelerate**.

- We then create a new class called **Bike**, inherited from the abstract class **Vehicle**, but with its own constructor.

- We then override the abstract method **decelerate** to use our own implementation.

Introduction to Programming in C#

> Using an abstract class just means that we list methods that would be useful for the children; however, the children will have to define how the method should be implemented.

The second way to implement dynamic polymorphism is by using **virtual** methods or variables. In the case of **virtual methods**, we declare a method that will be used by default by objects of this class or inherited classes; however, in this case, even if the method is ready to be used (i.e., because we have defined how it should be implemented), it can be changed (or overridden) by the child (i.e., the inherited class) to fit a specific purpose. In this case (i.e., inherited method), we need to specify that we override this method using the keyword **override**.

> The key difference between an abstract and a virtual method is that, while an abstract method should be overridden, a virtual methods may be overridden if the base method (i.e., the method declared in the base class) does not suit a particular purpose.

Let's look at an example:

```
class Vehicle
{
    protected float speed;
    public virtual void accelerate()
    {
        speed += 10;
    }
    public Vehicle(float newSpeed)
    {
        speed = newSpeed;
    }

}

class Bike : Vehicle
{
    public override void accelerate()
    {
        speed++;
    }
    public Bike(float newSpeed) : base(newSpeed){}

}
```

In the previous code:

- We declare a class **Vehicle**.

- It includes both a protected variable **speed** and a virtual method called **accelerate**. This method is virtual, which means that inherited classes will be able to modify (override) it, if need be.

- The class Bike has its own constructor; however, this constructor inherits from the parent's constructor; this means that by calling the constructor of the class Bike, we effectively call the parent's (of the base's) constructor, using the syntax:

```
public Bike(float newSpeed) : base(newSpeed){}
```

- We then create a new class **Bike** that inherits form the class **Vehicle**. In this class, we override the method accelerate using the keyword **override** so that the speed is just incremented by one.

WORKFLOW TO CREATE A SCRIPT

There are many ways to create and use scripts in Unity, but generally the process is as follows:

- Create a new script using the **Project** view (**Create | C# Script**) or the main menu (**Assets | Create | C# Script**).

- Attach the script to an object (e.g., drag and drop the script on the object).

- Check in the **Console** window that there are no errors in the script.

- Play the scene.

When you create your script, by default, the name of the class within the script will be the name of the script. So let's say that you created a new script called **TestCode**, then the following code will be automatically generated within:

```
using UnityEngine;
using System.Collections;

public class TestCode : MonoBehaviour
{
      public void Start ()
      {
      }
      public void Update ()
      {
      }
}
```

In the previous code, the class **TestCode** has been created; it inherits from the class **MonoBehaviour**, and it includes two methods that can be modified: **Start** and **Update**. You will also notice the two namespaces **UnityEngine** and **System.Collections**. As we have seen earlier, the keywords **using** is called a directive; in this particular case it is used to import what is called a namespace; put simply, by adding this directive you are effectively importing a collection of classes or data types. Each of these namespaces or "libraries" includes useful classes for your programme. For example the namespace **UnityEngine** will include classes for Unity development and **System.Collections** will include classes and interfaces, for different collections of objects. You can of course create classes that will not be linked to any object, and used to instantiate new objects.

HOW SCRIPTS ARE COMPILED

Whenever you create and save a script it is compiled and Unity will notify you (using the **Console** window) of any error. This being said, the order in which the scripts are compiled depends on its location. First, the scripts located in the folders **Standard Assets**, **Pro Standard Assets or Plugins**, then the scripts located in **Standard Assets/Editor**, **Pro Assets/Editor** or **Plugins/Editor**, and then the scripts outside the **Editor** folder, followed by the scripts in the **Editor** folder. For more information on script compilation, you can check the official documentation.

CODING CONVENTION

When you are coding, there are usually naming conventions based on the language that you are using. These often provide increased clarity for your code and depend on the language that you will be using.

Naming conventions usually employ a combination of camel casing and Pascal casing.

- In camel casing all words included in a name, except for the first one, is capitalized (e.g., myVariable).

- In Pascal casing all words included in a name are capitalized (e.g., MyVariable).

When coding in C# for example, naming conventions will use a combinations of camel an Pascal casing depending on whether you are naming a class, an interface, a variable or a resource.

However, as a C# beginner, in addition to learn about classes, methods, or inheritance, it may not be necessary to adhere completely to this naming convention at the start, at least as long as you use a consistent naming scheme.

So, while it is good to acknowledge different naming conventions for programming language and to understand why there are in place, and to keep things simple, this book will use a simplified naming convention, as follows:

- Classes (Pascal casing).

- All methods and variables (camel casing).

Once you feel comfortable with C# and want to know more about the official naming scheme, you may look at Microsoft official naming guidelines.

A FEW THINGS TO REMEMBER WHEN YOU CREATE A SCRIPT (CHECKLIST)

As you create your first scripts in the next chapter, there will be, without a doubt, errors and possibly hair pulling :-). You see, when you start coding, you will, as for any new activity, make small mistakes, learn what they are, improve your coding, and ultimately get better at writing your scripts. As I have seen students learning scripting, there are some common errors that are usually made; these don't make you a bad programmer; on the contrary, it is part of the learning process.

> We all learn by trial and error, and making mistakes is part of the learning process.

So, as you create your first script, set any fear aside, try to experiment, be curious, and get to learn the language. It is like learning a new foreign language: when someone from a foreign country understands your first sentences, you feel so empowered! So, it will be the same with C#, and to ease the learning process, I have included a few tips and things to keep in mind when writing your scripts, so that you progress even faster. You don't need to know all of these by now (I will refer to these later on, in the next chapter), but just be aware of it and also use this list if any error occurs (this list is also available as a pdf file in the resource pack, so that you can print it and keep it close by). So, watch out for these :-).

- Each opening bracket has a corresponding closing bracket.

- All variables are written consistently (e.g., spelling and case). The name of each variable is case-sensitive; this means that if you declare a variable **myvariable** but then refer to it as **myVariable** later on in the code, this may trigger an error, as the variable **myVariable** and **myvariable**, because they have a different case (upper- or lower-case **V**), are seen as two different variables.

- All variables are declared (type and name) prior to being used (e.g., **int**).

- The type of the argument passed to a method is the type that is required by this method.

- The type of the argument returned by a method is the type that is required to be returned by this method.

- Built-in functions are spelt with the proper case (e.g., upper-case **U** for **Update**).

- Use **camel casing** (i.e., capitalize the first character of each word except for the first word) or **Pascal casing** (i.e., capitalize the first character of each word) consistently.

- All statements are ended with a semi-colon.

- For **if** statements the condition is within round brackets.

- For **if** statements the condition uses the syntax "==" rather than "=".

- When calling a method, the exact name of this method (i.e., case-sensitive) is used.

- When referring to a variable, it is done with regards to the access type of the variable (e.g., public or private).

- Local variables are declared and can be used within the same method.

- Global variables are declared outside methods and can be used anywhere within the class.

2
CREATING YOUR FIRST SCRIPT

In this section we will start to code C# scripts in Unity. Some of the objectives of this section will be to:

- Introduce C# scripting in Unity.
- Explain some basic scripting concepts.
- Explain how to display information from the code to the **Console** window.

After completing this chapter you will be able to:

- Understand basic concepts in C#.
- Understand best coding practices.
- Code your first script in Unity.
- Create classes, methods and variables.
- Instantiate objects based on your own classes.
- Use built-in methods.
- Use conditional statements.

You can skip this chapter if you are already familiar with C#, or if you have already created and used C# scripts within Unity.

GETTING STARTED

In Unity, a script (C# script) is usually linked to an object; although it can also be used as a standalone class to be instantiated at a later stage; generally, for your script to be executed, it will need to be linked to an object. So to start with, we will create an empty object, create a script, and link this script to the object.

- Please launch Unity.
- Create a new Project (**File | New Project**).
- Create a new scene (**File | New Scene**).
- Create an empty object (**GameObject | Create Empty**).
- Rename this object: **example_for_scripting** in the **Hierarchy** window. To do so, you can either right-click on this object and then select the option **Rename**, from the contextual menu, or select the object (i.e., click once on it) and press *CTRL + Enter*.
- You will notice, looking at the **Inspector** window, that this object has only one component (**Transform**).

Let's create a new script:

- In the **Project** window, click once on the **Assets** folder.
- Create a new folder to store the scripts (this is not compulsory but it will help to organize your scripts): Select **Create | Folder**.

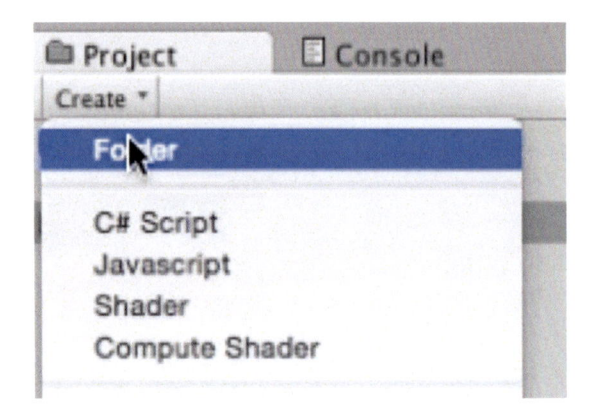

Figure 2-1: Creating a new folder

- This will create a new folder labeled **Folder**.

Creating your First Script

- Rename this folder **Scripts**.

- Double click on this folder to display its content and so that the script that we are about to create is added to this folder.

- In the **Project** window, select **Create | C# Script**.

- This should create a new **C#** script.

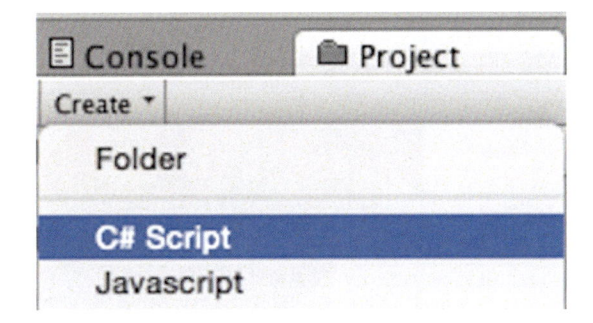

Figure 2-2: Creating a new C# script

- By default, this script will be named **NewBehaviourScript**. However, the name will be highlighted in blue so that you modify the name before the content of the script is created. Please rename this script **MyFirstScript**.

> Note that the name of the script should always match the name of the main class within the script; so if you want to rename this script later on, you will also need to modify the name of the main class within the script.

- Click once on the script; as you do so, look at the **Inspector** window, and you will see the content of the script. By default, you will notice that it includes a definition for the class **MyFirstScript**, namespaces, as well as two different member methods **Start** and **Update**.

- Double-click on the script (within the **Project** window), this will open the script in **MonoDevelop**, which is the default editor for Unity.

> Note that you can change to the editor of your choice (e.g., Notepad++ or Sublime). This can be done by changing Unity's preferences (**Edit | Preferences | External Tool**). This being said, while Mono Develop provides code auto completion by default, this may not be the case for other code editors (e.g., with Sublime, you need to install a specific package).

- As the script is opened in Mono Develop we can see it in more detail. Again, the **Start** method is called at the start of the scene, once. The method **Update** is called every time the screen is refreshed (every frame).

Creating your First Script

- These functions are case-sensitive; because they are built-in functions (i.e., functions made available by Unity for your use), Unity is expecting them to be spelt with the exact spelling and case; otherwise, it will assume that the method that you write serves a different purpose (i.e., we will come back to this type of error later-on).

So let's start coding.

- First let's create a variable of type **integer** called **number** as a private member variable.
- Type the following code just before the method **Start**:

```
private int number;
```

- As you can see, the variable is declared outside any method but inside the class **MyFirstScript**, which means that it is a member variable. The access modifier **private** specifies that the variable is accessible only by the class **MyFirstScript**.

- Then, we can declare a **String** variable called **myName**. Type the following code just after the previous declaration.

```
private string myName;
```

- Then type the following code inside the method **Start** (i.e., anywhere within its curly brackets).

```
number = 1;
```

- This code sets the variable **number** to 1; this variable was declared at the start of the script, as a member variable and it can be accessed from anywhere within the class **MyFirstScript**, including from inside the method **Start**.

- Then type the following code inside the method **Start** after the previous statement (you can replace the word **Patrick** with your own name if you wish):

```
myName = "Patrick";
```

- As you type this line, make sure that the name of the variable is spelt properly with proper case (i.e., upper-case **N**).

- Then type the following code after the previous statement to display a message in the **Console** window.

```
print ("Hello" + myName + "Your number is "+number);
```

- This should print the message **"Hello Patrick Your number is 1"** in the **Console** window in Unity. This window displays error messages from Unity or messages from the code. You may notice the quotes around the word **Patrick**, this means that the text **Hello** will be displayed and we will add the value of the variable **myName** to it. So these two strings will be concatenated (i.e., grouped) to form a dynamic sentence for which the content will depend on the value of the variables **myMame** and **number**.

So at this stage, your code should look as follows (and if it doesn't, you can use the next code snippet as a template):

```csharp
using UnityEngine;
using System.Collections;
public class MyFirstScript : MonoBehaviour
{
    // Use this for initialization
    private int number;
    private string name;
    void Start ()
    {
        number = 1;
        myName = "Patrick";
        print ("Hello"+ myName + "Your number is "+number);
    }
    // Update is called once per frame
    void Update ()
    {

    }
}
```

- At this stage, we can save our script (*CTRL + S*) and go back to Unity (*ALT + TAB*).

- In Unity, drag and drop the script **MyFirstScript** onto the empty object **example_for_scripting**, as illustrated on the next figure.

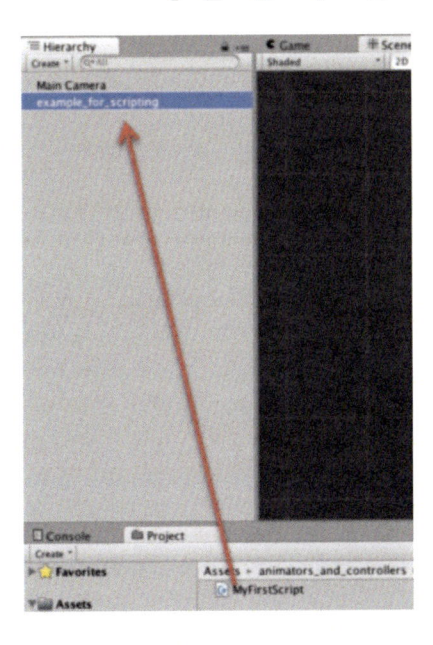

Figure 2-3: Linking the script to an object

Creating your First Script

- After this, if you click on the object **example_for_scripting** in the hierarchy, you should now see in the **Inspector** window that the script has become a component of this object.

- Look at the **Console** window to see if there are any errors; the window should be empty (i.e., no errors). If there are any warnings, you can leave them for the time being (it won't stop the scene from playing).

- We can now play the scene (*CTRL + P*); as we play the scene and look at the **Console** window (*SHIFT + CTRL + C*), we should see the message "**Hello Patrickyour number is 1**".

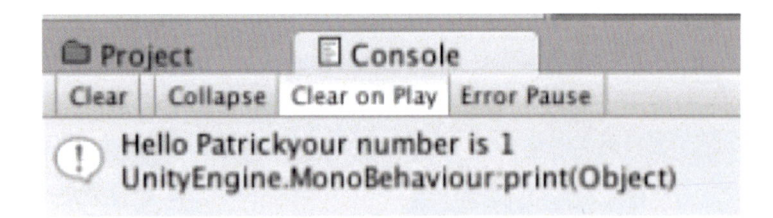

Figure 2-4: Displaying a message in the Console window - part 1

- You may notice a missing space between the words **Patrick** and **you**, and we can correct this accordingly. To do so, we can go back to your code editor (e.g., **Mono Develop**) to modify the script and add spaces as follows (after the words **Hello** and **is,** and before the word **your**):

```
print("Hello " + myName + " your number is "+number);
```

> As we go back to Unity, we can clear the **Console** window by clicking on the tab called **Clear**, as highlighted on the next figure. However, so that the **Console** window is cleared every time we run the scene, we can also click on the tab labeled **Clear on Play**. This ensures that the **Console** window is cleared every time the scene is played, avoiding cluttering the **Console** window with messages that may be obsolete or irrelevant.

- As we play the scene, we can see that the message has been modified to include a space between the words **Patrick** and **your**.

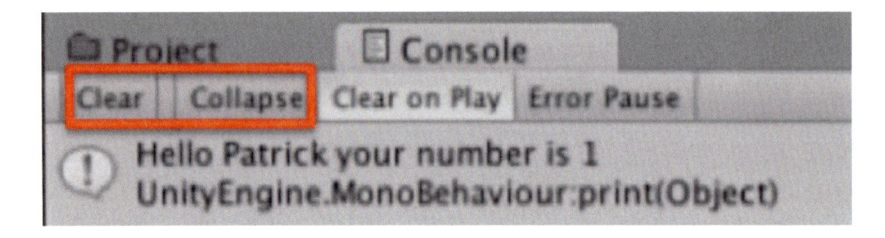

Figure 2-5: Displaying a message in the console window - part 2

Creating your First Script

This is it! We have created our first script using the built-in method **Start** and some variables, more specifically global variables. These variables are of type **integer** and **String**. Again, these variables are global as they were declared at the start of the script and outside any method. They can, as a result, be used across the script. The full script should look as described on the next code snippet.

```
using UnityEngine;
using System.Collections;
public class MyFirstScript : MonoBehaviour
{
    // Use this for initialization
    private int number;
    private string myName;

    void Start ()
    {
        number = 1;
        myName = "Patrick";
        print("Hello "+ myName + "Your number is " +number);
    }
    // Update is called once per frame
    void Update ()
    {

    }
}
```

USING THE UPDATE FUNCTION

Let's now use the method **Update** to display another message in the **Console** window. Again, this method is called every frame (i.e., every time the screen is refreshed), so any message printed within this method will be displayed indefinitely and every frame.

- Switch to Unity.

- Double click on the script **MyFirstScript** to open it.

- In **Mono Develop** (or any other code editor of your choice), type the following code within the curly brackets of the method **Update**:

```
print (myName);
```

- Save your code (*CTRL + S* or *APPLE + S* for Mac users).

- Switch to Unity and play the scene (*CTRL + P*).

[63]

Creating your First Script

- You should see that the message **Patrick** (or your own name) is displayed indefinitely. In the next figure, we can see that the message is displayed 148 times after a few seconds.

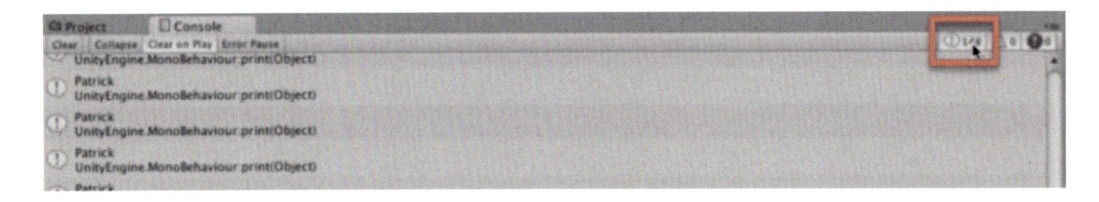

Figure 2-6: Using the "Collapse" option – part 1

- So the code is working well; however, because the message is displayed so many times, we have lost sight of the first message displayed from the **Start** function. This is because the console is flooded by hundreds of identical messages, and we could, to clear up the console, click on the tab labeled **Collapse** within the **Console** window.

> The **Collapse** option ensures that identical messages are displayed only once, along with a number that indicates how many times they have been listed.

- If we stop the game, press the **Collapse** option, and play the scene again, the **Console** window should look as described in the following figure.

Figure 2-7: Using the "Collapse" option - part 2

- As we can see, the message from the **Start** method is displayed (once), whereas the message from the **Update** method is displayed once but the consoles indicates that it has been issued 223 times.

CREATING LOCAL VARIABLES

At this stage, the code is working well, and we have created two member variables: **number** and **myName**. These two variables are accessible throughout our class; however, to experiment with local variables, we could also create variables that are only accessible from one method. So let's experiment.

- Switch back to your code editor (e.g., Mono Develop).

- Delete or comment the code we have just created in the **Update** function. To comment code, you can use double forward slashes, as described in the next code snippet.

Creating your First Script

```
//print (myName);
```

- Add the following code to the method **Start**, just before the closing bracket for this function.

```
int localVariable = 3;
print("local variable: "+localVariable);
```

With the first statement, we declare a variable that should only be used locally, that is to say, within the method **Start**. We then print the value of this variable and display a message that includes the string **"local variable"** that will be followed by (or appended to) the value of the variable **localVariable**; in our case, this should display **"local variable: 3"**.

- Check the code that you have written and ensure that it is correct (e.g., semi-colon at the end of each line).

- Save your script.

- Switch back to Unity and play the scene.

- As we play the scene, the **Console** window should look like the following:

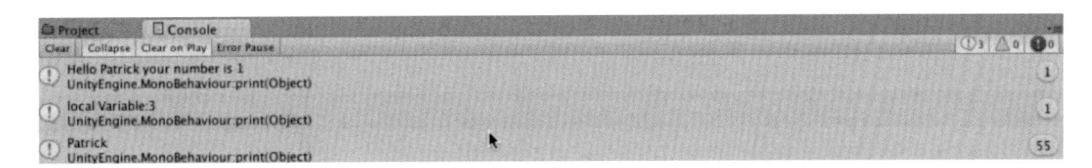

Figure 2-8: Displaying a local variable in the Console window

- We can see the first message from the **Start** method along with the second message that we have just created. Then the message from the **Update** method is displayed (55 times at this stage).

- Now, just to demonstrate the importance of variable scope, we will make an error on purpose; we will try to use the variable **myVariable** (which is a local variable) outside the method **Start**, where it has initially been declared. As you may have guessed, this should trigger an error.

- Switch back to **Mono Develop**.

- Type or copy and paste the following code inside the method **Update**.

```
print("local variable: "+localVariable);
```

- Save your script (*CTRL + S*).

- Switch back to Unity. Before you can try to play the scene, you will notice an error in the **Console** window as follows.

[65]

Creating your First Script

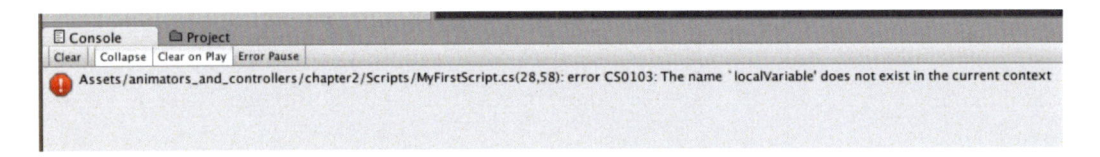

![Console error screenshot: Assets/animators_and_controllers/chapter2/Scripts/MyFirstScript.cs(28,58): error CS0103: The name 'localVariable' does not exist in the current context]

Figure 2-9: Generating an error on purpose

> By displaying this message, Unity is telling us that it does not recognize the variable **localVariable** in the context where it is being used. This is because it was declared locally in the **Start** method and then used outside this method. So if you see similar messages as you code your game, always check the scope of your variable. This should save you some headaches. :-)

- Switch back to your code editor and comment or delete the line we just created in the **Update** method.

```
//print("local variable "+localVariable);
```

> In C# you can comment a line of code by adding // to the start of the line. This means that the code will be part of the script, but it will not be executed.

CREATING A SIMPLE COUNTER

Let's create a simple counter to practice declaring and assigning values to variables. This timer will just count from 0 onwards and use a variable for which the value will be increased overtime (i.e., every frame).

- Switch back to Unity by pressing *ALT + Tab (or CMD + Tab* for Mac users*)*.

> As you will have to switch from Unity to **Mono Develop** (or another code editor) a couple of times during development, you can use this shortcut to do so, and it will save you a good bit of time. Imagine saving three seconds 300 times a day! So by pressing *ALT + Tab* (or *APPLE + Tab* on a Mac computer) you can switch back to the previous window (or the application that you were using). By keeping *ALT* pressed and then successively pressing the tab key several times, you can see and select the applications that are currently running on your computer.

- Add the following line at the top of our class (i.e., **MyFirstScript**) to declare our counter (just after the declaration for **myName**).

```
private int counter;
```

- Then, initialize the variable **counter** to **zero** by adding the following code within the **Start** method.

Creating your First Script

```
counter = 0;
```

> Note that this is done in the **Start** method only for now, so that it is done only once (i.e., at the start of the scene). If we were to add this code to the **Update** method instead, the variable would be initialized to 0 every frame (constantly), and we don't want this right now.

- Finally, add the following code at the end of the **Update** method so that we add one to the current value of the variable **counter** every frame (i.e., every time the screen is refreshed) and display its value.

```
counter = counter + 1;
print ("counter="+counter);
```

- After you have made these modifications, the code should look as follows:

```csharp
using UnityEngine;
using System.Collections;
public class MyFirstScript : MonoBehaviour
{
    // Use this for initialization
    private int number;
    private string myName;
    private int counter;

    void Start ()
    {
        number = 1;
        myName = "Patrick";
        print("Hello "+ myName + "Your number is " +number);

        int localVariable = 3;
        print("local variable: "+localVariable);
        counter = 0;
    }

    // Update is called once per frame
    void Update ()
    {
        counter = counter + 1;
        print ("counter="+counter);
    }
}
```

- Switch back to Unity (*ALT + TAB*).

Creating your First Script

- Look at the **Console** window: it should not display any error (i.e., provided that you have commented or deleted the code that we created to generate an error on purpose).

- Play the scene (*CTRL + P*), look at the **Console** window, and you should see that the value of the counter is displayed and that it is increasing.

> You may notice that, even if you press the **Collapse** option in the **Console** window, the messages are not collapsed and that they still flood the **Console** window. This is because the **Collapse** option works only when the exact same message is displayed several times; however, in our case, the message differs every frame as the value of the counter is different every time (e.g., "counter=1", "counter=2", etc.).

At this stage we know about local and global variables, so let's look into methods and create our very first method.

CREATING YOUR FIRST METHOD

So what is a method? A method (what we used to call function in JavaScript) is usually employed to perform a task outside the main body of the game. I usually compare functions to a friend or a colleague to whom you gently ask to perform a task for you. In many cases you will call them and they will perform the task. Sometime they will need some particular information to perform the task (e.g., a number to be able to call someone on your behalf); some other times, they will call you back to give you the information that they found, but in other cases, this may not be necessary, and they will perform the task without contacting you afterwards.

So there are essentially three types of methods:

- Methods that just perform actions with no parameters.
- Methods that perform actions with parameters.
- Methods that perform actions (with or without a parameter) and return a result.

DECLARING A METHOD

If you have coded in JavaScript before, functions were declared using the keyword **function**; however, in C# a method declaration usually requires an access modifier, the type of data returned, and the type of the parameters passed to this function.

The syntax to declare a method is as follows:

- The access modifier (e.g., private, public, or protected).
- The type of data returned by the method (e.g., **float**, **string** or **bool**).
- The name of the method.
- Opening round brackets.
- The type of the parameters and their name.
- Closing round brackets.
- Any action (i.e., statement) performed by this method will be added within the curly brackets and followed by a semi-colon.

In the next sections, we will see examples of how methods can be declared.

Creating your First Script

METHODS THAT DON'T RETURN OR TAKE ANY PARAMETER

In this case, the method is called with no parameter; it will then perform an action. This is the simplest form of methods. The syntax is as follows: the access modifier, the keyword **void**, followed by the **name of the function**, followed by **opening and closing round brackets**, followed by **opening and closing curly brackets**. Any action (i.e., statement) performed by this function will be added within the curly brackets and followed by a semi-colon.

```
public void theNameOfyourMethod()
{
}
```

The keyword **void** indicates that the method does not return any data.

So to create our first method, we could type the following at the end of our script (i.e., before the last closing curly brackets):

```
public void myFirstMethod()
{
    print ("Hello World");
}
```

When called, this method will print the message **"Hello World"** to the **Console** window.

At this stage we have just defined the method **myFirstMethod**; in other words, we have specified what the method should do when it has been called. So once the method has been defined, we can call it using the syntax: **nameOfTheMethod()**; for example, to call **myFirstMethod** from any other method within the script, we could write the following statement at the end of the **Start** method:

```
myFirstMethod();
```

So that this message stands out in the **Console** window, we can comment all other **print** statements inside the **Start** method so that the code of your script looks like this (the changes are highlighted in bold):

```
using UnityEngine;
using System.Collections;
public class MyFirstScript : MonoBehaviour
{
        // Use this for initialization
        private int number;
        private string myName;
        private int counter;

        void Start ()
        {
            number = 1;
            myName = "Patrick";
            //print("Hello "+ myName + "Your number is " +number);

            int localVariable = 3;
            //print("local variable: "+localVariable);
            counter = 0;
            myFirstMethod();
        }

        // Update is called once per frame
        void Update ()
        {
            counter = counter + 1;
            //print ("counter="+counter);


        }
        public void myFirstMethod()
        {
            print ("Hello World");
        }
}
```

Creating your First Script

> You may wonder why the methods **Update** and **Start** do not include any access modifier (e.g., public or private). This is because by default, the access modifier for a member method in C# is private. So if no access modifier is specified for a method, it will be treated as a private method.
>
> Note that the location of the method in the script (i.e., at the end or at the start) does not matter, as long as it is declared within the class (**MyFirstScript**) and outside any another method: so you need to declare your method outside of any other methods (i.e., after the closing curly bracket for a method or before the method); we could have easily written this method at the start or middle of the script, resulting in no errors.

- Check that your code is written properly (i.e., error-free).
- Save your code (*CTRL + S*).
- Switch to Unity (*ALT + TAB*).
- Check that there are no errors in the **Console** window.
- Play the scene and check that the message says **"Hello World"**.

DEFINING A METHOD THAT TAKES PARAMETERS

So far, we looked at methods that would not take or return any parameters. For now, we will create a method that still doesn't return any data, but that takes one or several parameters in order to perform calculations.

So to borrow the previous example, you call someone, give them some information, and ask them to perform an action based on your instructions. To illustrate this concept, let's create a new method that will display a message based on a parameter passed as an argument.

- Please type the following code at the end of the class (i.e., before the last closing curly bracket).

```
public void mySecondMethod(string name)
{
    print ("Hello, your name is " +name);
}
```

- In the previous code, we have created a method called **mySecondMethod**. It takes a parameter called **name** of type **String** (i.e., text). So when we call this method and include a string variable within the brackets, this variable will be referred as **name** within this method.
- Let me illustrate with the following code.

Creating your First Script

```
mySecondMethod("Patrick");
```

If we were to type the previous code inside the **Start** method, the method **mySecondMethod** would set the variable **name** with the string **Patrick**, and then display the message **Hello Patrick**. The variable **name** is a local variable to the method **mySecondFunction**.

If you have not already done so, please add the following code to the **Start** method. You can replace the word **Patrick** with your own name.

```
mySecondMethod("Patrick");
```

- Save your code, switch to Unity, check the **Console** window for any error and play the scene.

- You should see, amongst other messages, the message **"Hello, your name is Patrick"**.

- You could now change the call to this method and pass your own name as a parameter and see the result as you play the scene.

Note that we could have created a method that takes many other parameters. For example, we could have created a method that takes the first and last names as parameters, as follows.

```
public void myThirdMethod(string fName, string lName)
{
    print ("Hello, your name is " +fName+" "+lName);
}
```

DEFINING A METHOD THAT TAKES PARAMETERS AND RETURNS INFORMATION

So far we know how to declare a method that takes parameters; however we have not yet seen how we could define a method that also returns information.

This type of method, will, in addition to possibly taking parameters and processing this information, return information back to where it was called.

In the following example, we will create a method that does all three: it will be called; it will then take the **year of birth** as a parameter, and then calculate and return the corresponding **age** (based on the current year).

- Please add the following code at the end of the script.

Creating your First Script

```
public int calculateAge(int YOB)
{
        int age;
        age = 2016 - YOB;
        return (age);
}
```

In the previous code:

- The method called **calculateAge** is declared using the keywords **public** and **int** as its access type is **public** and as it will return an **integer**.

- The method called **calculateAge** takes a parameter called **YOB** (short for Year Of Birth).

- The method **calculateAge** then subtracts **YOB** from the current year and returns the result.

Please add the following code to the method **Start**.

```
int myAge = calculateAge(1998);
print("Your age is " + myAge);
```

In the previous code:

- The method **calculateAge** is called once; it returns the calculated age, and this (returned) value is saved in the variable called **myAge**.

- This variable **myAge** is then printed in the **Console** window.

- Save your code, and switch back to Unity.

- Check that there are no errors in the **Console** window and play the scene.

- The console should display, amongst other messages, the message **"Your age is 18"**.

As you can see, there are different types of methods that you can create, depending on your needs. They may or may not take parameters, and they may or may not return values.

CREATING YOUR OWN CLASS

To complete this section, it would be great to see how you could create and use your own class. So, we will simply create a class for a bike and also use it. So, let's get started.

- Please create a new C# script called **Bike** (i.e., select **Create | C# Script** from the **Project** window).

- This should generate a script with the following code by default:

```
using UnityEngine;
using System.Collections;

public class Bike : MonoBehaviour {

    // Use this for initialization
    void Start () {

    }

    // Update is called once per frame
    void Update () {

    }
}
```

When this is done, let's edit this script to add some features to our bike.

- We can start by deleting the text **:MonoBehaviour**. This is because our class will be used as a standalone and not inherit from the **MonoBehaviour** class (which is mainly for game objects in the scene).

- Then we can delete the methods Start and Update, for the same reason as explained above, as we will create our own methods for our class Bike.

- So your code should look like the following:

Creating your First Script

```
using UnityEngine;
using System.Collections;

public class Bike
{


}
```

At this stage we have a blank canvas that we can use for our new class.

- Please add the following code at the start of the class (just before the comment "**Use this for initialization**"). The new code is highlighted in bold.

```
using UnityEngine;
using System.Collections;

public class Bike
{
    private string name;
    private float speed;
    private int nbWheels;

}
```

- In the previous code, we declare three private member variables of type **string**, **float** and **int**. These will be used to identify the name, speed and number of wheels for the bike created.

We now need to define one or more constructors for our class, to define the feature of each new bike created. Please add the following code within the class:

```
//First Constructor
public Bike()
{
        name = "Just another bike";
        speed = 0.0f;
}
//Second Constructor
public Bike(string newName)
{
        name = newName;
        speed = 0.0f;
        Debug.Log ("Just created a new bike with the name" + name);

}
```

- In the previous code, we create two constructors; both methods are public and their names are the same as the name of our class (i.e., Bike).

The method **print** that we used earlier is only accessible for classes that inherit from the class **MonoBehaviour**; in our case, we have removed this inheritance (our class does not inherit anymore from the class **MonoBehaviour**), so we use the method **Debug.Log** instead which is accessible from the library **UnityEngine** that we imported at the start of our script); this is equivalent to the method **print**.

- The first constructor will be used if the object is created but no parameters are used at its instantiation. We see that, by default, we just set the name of this bike to "**Just another bike**" and its speed to **0**. This constructor will be called if we use the following code to create a new bike.

```
Bike bike1 = new Bike();
```

- The next constructor takes a **string** as a parameter; which means that it will be called if we create a new bike and pass a string as a parameter when an object is created from this class (i.e., instantiated). We see that if this is the case, the name of the bike will be set to (or initialized with) the parameter passed to this constructor and its speed will be set to **0**. This constructor will be called if we use the following code to create a new bike.

```
Bike bike2 = new Bike("Name of the Bike");
```

So your code should look like the following by now (if not, you can use the next code as a template).

Creating your First Script

```
using UnityEngine;
using System.Collections;

public class Bike
{
    private string name;
    private float speed;
    private int nbWheels;

    //First Constructor
    public Bike()
    {
        name = "Just another bike";
        speed = 0.0f;
    }
    //Second Constructor
    public Bike(string newName)
    {
        name = newName;
        speed = 0.0f;
        Debug.Log ("Just created a new bike with the name " + name);
    }
}
```

So, once you have created our new class, we could now test it by doing the following:

- Open the script **MyFirstScript**.
- Add the following code in the **Start** method.

```
Bike b1 = new Bike ("My First Bike");
```

- Save your script.
- Play the scene.
- You should see that the **Console** window displays the message **"Just created a new bike with the name My First Bike"**.

So at this stage, while we have created constructors, we could also create methods that make it possible to modify some of the attributes of our bike.

For example, we could add the following method to the class **Bike**.

Creating your First Script

```
public void accelerate ()
{
        speed+=1;
        Debug.Log ("Our new speed is now" + speed);
}
```

We can then modify the **Start** method in the script MyFirstScript as follows (new code in bold).

```
Bike b1 = new Bike ("My First Bike");
```
b1.accelerate();
b1.accelerate();

Save this code, and play the scene. You should see two additional messages in the **Console** window saying **"Our new speed is now 1"** and **"Our new speed is now 2"**.

COMMON ERRORS AND THEIR MEANING

As you will start your journey through C# coding, you may sometimes find it difficult to interpret the errors produced by Unity in the console. However, after some practice, you will manage to recognize them, to understand (and also avoid) them, and to fix them accordingly. The next list identifies the errors that my students often come across when they start coding in C#.

When an error occurs, Unity usually provides you with enough information to check where it has occurred, so that you can fix it. While many are relatively obvious to spot, some others are trickier to find. In the following, I have listed some of the most common errors that you will come across as you start with C#. The trick is to recognize the error message so that you can understand what Unity is trying to tell you. Again, this is part of the learning process, and you **WILL** make these mistakes, but as you see these errors, you will learn to understand them (and avoid them too :-)). Again, Unity is trying to help you by communicating, to the best that it can, where the issue is; by understanding the error messages we can get to fix these bugs easily. So that it is easier to fix errors, Unity usually provides the following information when an error occurs:

- Name of the script where the error was found.

- The number of the row and column where the error was found.

- A description of the error that was found.

So, if Unity was to generate the following message **"Assets/Scripts/MyFirstScript.cs (23,34) BCE0085: Unknown identifier: 'localVariable'"**, it is telling us that an error has occurred in the script called **MyFirstScript**, at the line **23**, and around the **34th** character (i.e., column) on this line. In this particular message, it is telling us that it can't recognize the variable **localVariable**.

So, you may come across the following errors (this list is also available in the resource pack as a pdf file, so that you can print it and keep it close by):

- **";" expected**: This error could mean that you have forgotten to add a semi-colon at the end of a statement. To fix this error, just go to the line mentioned in the error message and ensure that you add a semi-colon.

- **Unknown identifier**: This error could mean that Unity does not know the variable that you are mentioning. It can be due to at least three reasons: (1) the variable has not been declared yet, (2) the variable has been declared but outside the scope of the method (e.g., declared locally in a different function), or (3) the name of the variable that you are using is incorrect (i.e., spelling or case). Remember, the names of all variables and functions are case-sensitive; so by just using an incorrect case, Unity will assume that you refer to another variable, which, in this case, has not been declared yet.

- **The best method overload for function ... is not compatible**: This error is probably due to the fact that you are trying to call a function and to pass a parameter with a type that is not what Unity is expecting. For example, the method **mySecondMethod**, described in the next code snippet, is expecting a **String** value for its parameter; so, if you pass an integer value instead, an error will be generated.

```
void mySecondFunction(string name)
{
    print ("Hello, your name is" +name);
}
mySecondFunction("John");//this is correct
mySecondFunction(10);//this will trigger an error
```

- **Expecting } found ...:** This error is due to the fact that you may have forgotten to either close or open curly brackets. This can be the case for conditional statements or functions. To avoid this issue, there is a trick (or best practice) that you can use: you can ensure that you indent your code so that corresponding opening and closing brackets are at the same level. In the next example, you can see that the brackets corresponding to the start and end of the method **testBrackets** are indented at the same level, and so are the brackets for each of the conditional statements within this function. By indenting your code (using several spaces or tabulation), you can make sure that your code is clear and that missing curly brackets are easier to spot.

```
Void testBrackets()
{
    if (myVar == 2)
    {
        print ("Hello World");
        myVar = 4;
    }
    else
    {
    }
}
```

Sometimes, although the syntax of your code is correct and does not yield any error in the **Console** window, it looks like nothing is happening; in other words, it looks like the code, and especially the methods that you have created do not work. This is bound to happen as you create your first scripts. It can be quite frustrating (and I have been there :-)) because, in this case, Unity will not let us know where the error is. However, there is a succession of checks that you can perform to ensure that this does not happen; so you could check the following:

- The script that you have written has been saved.
- The script has no errors.
- The script is attached to an object.
- If the script is indeed attached to an object and you are using a built-in method that depends on the type of object it is attached to, make sure that the script is linked to the correct object. For example, if your script is using the built-in method

OnControllerColliderHit, which is used to detect collision between the **FPSController** and other objects, but you don't drag and drop the script on the **FPSController** object, the script, while being error-free, will not be used, and the method **OnControllerColliderHit** will not be called if you collide with an object.

- If the script is indeed attached to the right object and is using a built-in method such as **Start**, or **Update**, make sure that these functions are spelt properly (i.e., exact spelling and case). For example for the method **Update**, what happens here is that the system will call the method **Update** every frame, and no other function. So if you write a method spelt **update**, the system will look for the **Update** function, and since it has not been defined (or overwritten), nothing will happen, unless you specifically call this function. The same would happen for the method **Start**. In both cases, the system will assume that you have created two new functions **update** and **start**.

BEST PRACTICES

To ensure that your code is easy to understand and that it does not generate countless headaches when trying to modify it, there are a few good practices that you can start applying as your begin with coding; these should save you some time along the line.

Variable naming

- Use meaningful names that you can understand, especially after leaving your code for two weeks.

```
string myName = "Patrick";//GOOD
string b = "Patrick";//NOT SO GOOD
```

- Capitalize words within a name consistently (e.g., camel or Pascal casing).

```
bool testIfTheNameIsCorrect;// GOOD
bool testifthenameiscorrect; // NOT SO GOOD
```

Methods

- Check that all opening brackets have a corresponding closing bracket.

- Indent your code.

- Comment your code as much as possible to explain how it works.

- Use the **Start** method if something just needs to be done once at the start of the game.

- If something needs to be done repeatedly, then the method **Update** might be a better option.

3 FREQUENTLY ASKED QUESTIONS

This chapter provides answers to the most frequently asked questions about the features that we have covered in this book. Please also note that some videos are also available on the companion site to help you with some of the concepts covered in this topic, including AI, UI, collision, cameras, or paths.

C# SCRIPTS

How do I create a script?

In the **Project** window, select: **Create | C# Script**.

How can my script be executed?

As for JavaScript scripts, your C# script may need to be attached to an object. This being said, you could also create a class that is not linked to an object but that is used indirectly by another class (that could be attached to an object).

How can I check that my script has no errors?

Open the **Console** window and any error should be displayed here.

What is object-oriented programming?

In object-oriented programming, your program is seen as a collection of objects that interact with each other using, for example, methods.

Should the name of my C# file and the containing class within be the same?

When you create a new C# file, Unity will let you rename it straight-away; once this is done, it will automatically generate the name of the class within, using the name that you have specified for this file. So, if you happened to change the name of this file later on, you may also need to change the name of the class within.

Why should I use C#?

There are several good reasons to start coding in C#. One of them is that C# is an object-oriented programming language that is relatively similar to other languages such as Java. So by learning C# you should be able to transfer this knowledge to other languages easily.

What is the dot notation for?

The dot notation refers to **object-oriented programming**. Using dots, you can access properties and functions (or methods) related to a particular object. For example **gameObject.transform.position** gives you access to the **position** from the **transform** of the object linked to a script. It is often useful to read it backward; in this case, the dot can be interpreted as **"of"**. So in our case, **gameObject.transform.position** can be translated as "the position **of** the transform **of** the **gameObject**".

4
THANK YOU

I would like to thank you for completing this book; I trust that you are now comfortable with C#. This book is of course only a quick guide to get started with Unity; if you'd like to know more about Unity, you may try some of my other books available from the official page: http://www.learntocreategames.com/books.

So that the book can be constantly improved, I would really appreciate your feedback and hear what you have to say. So, please leave me a helpful review on Amazon letting me know what you thought of the book and also send me an email (learntocreategames@gmail.com) with any suggestion you may have. I read and reply to every email.

Thanks so much!!

Made in the USA
San Bernardino, CA
18 July 2018